T0334356

Cambridge Elements ≡

Elements in Feminism and Contemporary Critical Theory
edited by
Jennifer Cooke
Loughborough University
Amber Jamilla Musser
CUNY Graduate Center
Juno Jill Richards
Yale University

TRANSGENRE

Aaron Hammes
Case Western Reserve University

CAMBRIDGE
UNIVERSITY PRESS

Shaftesbury Road, Cambridge CB2 8EA, United Kingdom

One Liberty Plaza, 20th Floor, New York, NY 10006, USA

477 Williamstown Road, Port Melbourne, VIC 3207, Australia

314–321, 3rd Floor, Plot 3, Splendor Forum, Jasola District Centre,
New Delhi – 110025, India

103 Penang Road, #05–06/07, Visioncrest Commercial, Singapore 238467

Cambridge University Press is part of Cambridge University Press & Assessment,
a department of the University of Cambridge.

We share the University's mission to contribute to society through the pursuit
of education, learning and research at the highest international levels of excellence.

www.cambridge.org
Information on this title: www.cambridge.org/9781009502221

DOI: 10.1017/9781009502191

When citing this work, please include a reference to the DOI 10.1017/9781009502191

First published 2025

A catalogue record for this publication is available from the British Library

ISBN 978-1-009-50222-1 Hardback
ISBN 978-1-009-50221-4 Paperback
ISSN 2754-303X (online)
ISSN 2754-3021 (print)

Cambridge University Press & Assessment has no responsibility for the persistence
or accuracy of URLs for external or third-party internet websites referred to in this
publication and does not guarantee that any content on such websites is, or will
remain, accurate or appropriate.

TransGenre

Elements in Feminism and Contemporary Critical Theory

DOI: 10.1017/9781009502191
First published online: January 2025

Aaron Hammes
Case Western Reserve University
Author for correspondence: Aaron Hammes, ahammes@gradcenter.cuny.edu

Abstract: *TransGenre* is a reconsideration of genre theory in long-form fiction through transgender minor literature in the US and Canada. Using four genre sites (the road novel, the mourning novel, the chosen family novel, and the archival novel), this Element considers how the minoritized becomes the minoritarian through deterritorializing generic conventions in fiction to its own ends. In so doing, *TransGenre* proposes narrative reading practices as strategies of the minor to subvert, transgress, and reappropriate the novel's genealogy and radical future prospects. A range of fiction published in the past decade is deployed as largely self-theorizing, generating its own epistemological, thematic, and formal innovations and possibilities, revealing cisheteronormative underpinnings of generic categories and turning them in on themselves.

Keywords: transgender literature, transfeminism, deterritorialization, minor literature, queer and trans studies

ISBNs: 9781009502221 (HB), 9781009502214 (PB), 9781009502191 (OC)
ISSNs: 2754-303X (online), 2754-3021 (print)

Contents

1 TransGenre

"Tragedy can become comedy, but then it can jump back to being tragic again. Plus, real life often defies genre."

(Plante, *Any Other City*, 38)

"How many styles or genres or literary movements, even very small ones, have only one single dream: to assume a major function in language."

(Deleuze and Guattari, *Kafka: Toward a Minor Literature*, 27)

"I suggest constituting transsexuals not as a class or problematic 'third gender,' but rather as a genre – a set of embodied texts whose potential for productive disruption of structured sexualities and spectra of desire has yet to be explored."

(Stone, "The Empire Strikes Back," 231)

Genre as narrative category or convention, genre as the dream of a major enunciative function, genre as a textual kinship and stand-in for gender. Hazel Jane Plante's novel *Any Other City* is a fictionalized memoir, complete with a frame narrative detailing how the author was connected with famous punk singer Tracy St. Cyr after the publication of Plante's first novel, *Little Blue Encyclopedia (for Vivian)* (featured in the mourning novel section of this Element). The novel/memoir is laid out like an album, complete with "A" and "B" sides, troubling form, genre, and even medium as Tracy's story is mediated by the author within the narrative structure, as well as the "real" Plante, toiling at her second novel. Real life defies genre, but how we understand it is structured by genre as well. Nearly half a century earlier, Deleuze and Guattari, in *Kafka: Toward a Minor Literature*, work through the unique and the exemplary in the work of Franz Kafka, in part through considering ways in which genre readings fail to comprehend his corpus: novels, aphorisms, letters, diaries, stories – most of it unpublished during his lifetime. Dreaming of the major whilst operating from and through the minor may describe Kafka's desire to be read alongside Goethe and Schiller as well as Deleuze and Guattari's drive to excavate a different modality in Kafka's aesthetic production. A minor function is not one strictly of diminutive scale; it is instead the enactment of dreams of the majoritarian for minoritarian uses. Finally, (chronologically) halfway between Deleuze and Guattari's philosophy and Plante's fiction is Sandy Stone's foundational document of contemporary trans studies, "The Empire Strikes Back," both a response to a transphobic turn in radical feminist philosophy and a meditation on transgender embodiment and epistemology. Stone uses genre as an alternative to binary gender, both a potential for disruption and the sense of sex–gender as a spectrum. Each of these notes on genre is an opportunity for a trans interlocution of feminist discourse; transfeminism is itself a genre that is not simply expanded to include trans subjects and their narratives, but rather one that takes seriously minor uses and remapping of extant generic resources. In these ways, transgeneric reading is transfeminist reading, seeking not simply representation, but radical deterritorialization and minor uses of genre and form. *TransGenre* seeks to contour and allow to blossom various elements of genre, thinking with the capacities of contemporary anglophone North American transgender fiction to maneuver through, with, and against generic convention and stricture. In this introduction, I attempt to reflect the spirit of trans minor literature by offering some unfinished, at times aporetic meditations on some of the key concepts to follow. This initial inhalation is meant to suggest a minor reading practice that *TransGenre* proceeds to enact at four sites before concluding with a sense of what it means and what it could mean to read minor genre transgenerically.

The Minor

This Element operates from a sense of the minor as a mode of cultural production that both hails to minoritized communities and wields the language of the majoritarian for its own purposes. In their formative study on the possibilities of a minor literature, Deleuze and Guattari seek to detail the forms and functions of a literature that expresses the drive "to hate all the languages of the master" (26). The trans minor literature detailed in this Element troubles the boundaries of generic conventions while refusing to overtly reject them; it is minor in part through its referentiality to the major. Furthermore, I read Deleuze and Guattari's sense of minor literature as embodied and aspirational; what it moves toward in part is to "know how to create a becoming-minor" (27), as individuals both creating and reflected within the literature are always connected to larger communities. At each of the sites in this Element, community is thematized and tested, the minoritized becoming the minoritarian through community self-definition and flexibility. But Deleuze and Guattari have even more august ambitions for minor literature, perhaps grander than have been accounted for in the wake of their work. They seek after, in the figure of Kafka but certainly reaching beyond as well, the position from which "minor no longer designates specific literatures but the revolutionary conditions for every literature within the heart of what is called great (or established) literature" (18). These revolutionary conditions are as much survival and resistance tactics as aesthetic precepts, and gesture toward a station for literature that is inaccessible (which is not to preclude also being illegible and undesirable) to the great and established. I detail elsewhere "the specific ways in which this fiction deterritorializes the tropes, motifs, forms, and mechanics of the novel according to communitarian self-definition activates the revolutionary potential of the minor" (Hammes, "Minor Literature as Trans Literature," 448). This Element deploys genre reading as a means of further motivating these revolutionary conditions.

What the minor does for trans literature is offer a kinship of deterritorialization and resistance with minoritized literatures (including those we might understand as "feminized" (see Gill-Peterson, *A Short History of Trans Misogyny*) or "gender disruptive" (see Heyam, *Before We Were Trans*), if not retroactively "trans") of the past. While Deleuze and Guattari introduce the deterritorialization of Kafka's language as one suitable for "strange and minor uses" (17), I propose extending the concept into genre, form, and, to borrow Deleuze and Guattari's term, "function." The strange and minor uses that interest us here are those that deterritorialize generic conventions and offer new possibilities for reading and writing fiction. This minor key is the poignant diminution that subverts and transgresses great (and established) forms for its own purposes.

Genre

> "We intuitively know that everyday life doesn't conform to the simple outlines of well-made genres." (Milks, *Margaret and the Mystery of the Missing Body*, 255)

Genre is founded on difference and distinction. In full pedagogue–provocateur mode, Derrida writes in "The Law of Genre," "As soon as genre announces itself, one must respect a norm, one must not cross a line of demarcation, one must not risk impunity, anomaly, or monstrosity" (203). That said, Derrida's sense of genre law contains within itself "a principle of contamination" (204). The "Trans" of *TransGenre* is rooted in both transition and transgression, the sense of refusing, overwriting, or complicating the assignment of sex–gender at (and after) birth. The genre readings that follow attempt to sketch out both the laws of these genres and their contamination and deterritorialization. And as for "anomaly, or monstrosity," trans minor literature makes room for the appropriation of phobic majorities' sense of the monster, whether through the deployment of rage (see Stryker, "Frankenstein") or "reclamation" (Rosenberg, *Confessions of the Fox*, 84n). This monster lurks throughout each generic convention, the bad other by which the road, the family, mourning, and the archive are defined.

Derrida goes on to suggest that "genre has always in all genres been able to play the role of order's principle" (228), whether through "resemblance," "order of reasons," or "sense of history," among others. Though the law of genre can be thought of as "a participation without belonging – a taking part without being part of" (206), it remains the case that "there is no genreless text" (212). Trans minor literature is not a genre, in this accounting, but the minor is very much a "taking part without being part" of the majoritarian literary tradition. *TransGenre* seeks the points at which the principle of contamination becomes the locus of deterritorialization. When Derrida goes on to suggest that "the law of genre also has a controlling influence and is binding on that which draws the genre into engendering, generations, genealogy, and degenerescence" (221), he clears space for strange and minor uses that emerge from degenerescence and the reformation of generic conventions.

Literary genres are arguably the stuff of the major, or at the very least a heuristic to separate the major from the minor, defined equally by their norms and the latitude to deviate from them. Much of traditional literary genre studies works from principles of either genealogy/history or morphology/resemblance. Bawrashi and Reiff, in *Genre*, offer an instructive menu of these sorts of figurations of genre. They note, from David Fishelov's "analogies," genre as "literary institutions that make certain literary activities possible and meaningful, both in terms of the subjects who participate within them and in terms of the writers and readers who produce and interpret them" (18). Here, genres are both conditions of possibility and meaningfulness. Similar is Fredric Jameson's ("Magical Narratives") accounting of genres as literary institutions, social contracts specifying the "proper use" of cultural artifacts. This sociality is important for many writers around genre, and moves us closer to the more dynamic usage this Element deploys. Jonathan Culler ("Lyric, History, and Genre") cites genre as prerequisite for literary activity, declaring that writing is made possible by the existence of genre that can be written within or against. E. D. Hirsch writes of genre as constitutive rather than conditioning possibility, detailing genre as an interpretive framework that makes up a reader's understanding of a text, allowing for "conventionalized predictions or guesses" about a text (Bawrashi and Reiff, *Genre*, 23). These readings of genre resist accounting for it as strictly formal or thematic; they each propose genre as elemental to the experience of reading and legibility.

The fourth essay of Northrup Frye's *Anatomy of Criticism* gives pride of place to the concept in its title, "Rhetorical Criticism: Theory of Genres." Frye's conclusions can seem to relegate genre to pure rhetoric, but perhaps the "anatomy" as a whole attempts to revivify the functionality of rhetoric. Frye writes that "the generic distinctions are among the ways in which literary works are ideally presented, whatever the actualities are" (247). Trans minor literature cuts between ideality in its generic signposts and actuality in the lived experiences of its minoritized subjects. One can think of genre, and especially its minor uses, as a system of interrelationship – that is, in Wai Chee Dimock's

("Genre as World System") concept of "world system," a "self-obsoleting system, a provisional set that will always be bent and pulled and stretched by its many subsets"(86). Genre is "always on the verge of taking flight, in some unknown and unpredictable direction," and thus genre can be considered "not just a theory of classification" but "a theory of interconnection" (86). This interconnection is the transgeneric potential of the minor to hold together seemingly disparate municipalities of genre through signaling to minoritized communities and subjects.

Minor Genre

And so minor genre emerges from minoritarian interconnection, signaling within and between communities, across variations on minor subject positions. Carolyn R. Miller ("Genre as Social Action") suggests we pursue genre theory "because it emphasizes some social and historical aspects of rhetoric that other perspectives do not" (151). These aspects are expressed by centering genre not on "substance or the form of discourse" but on "the actions it is used to accomplish" (151). Put another way, "genre can be said to represent typified rhetorical action" (151). Minor literatures do not aim for universality, but in/through/against genre the minor attains both legibility and a means of smuggling in radical political potential in recognizable forms. Miller continues that among the ways that genre claims can fail is when "there is no pragmatic component, no way to understand the genre as social action" (164). Of course "social action" is both broad and subject to different readings (Is it opposed to individual or antisocial action? Or social inaction?). Miller clarifies: "As a recurrent, significant action, a genre embodies an aspect of cultural rationality. For the critic, genres can serve both as an index to cultural patterns and as tools for exploring the achievements of particular speakers and writers; for the student, genres serve as keys to understanding how to participate in the actions of a community" (165). *TransGenre* uses genre as a cipher for different functions of community action, not least minoritarian expression itself. Devitt offers a further gloss on genre and social action: "Being part of society enables individuals to change society, and hence to change genres, for genres, as Volosinov/Bakhtin writes, 'exhibit an extraordinary sensitivity to all fluctuations in the social atmosphere' ... " (see Emerson and Morson, *Mikhail Bakhtin*, 579), allowing one to "create and recreate the society" that genre "conventions reflect" (580). Reading for minor genre is an attunement to this sensitivity, calibrating fiction's (minor) capacities through genre play, distortion, disruption, and conformity. Bakhtin sees this use of genre as grounds for innovation on "genre conditions" (466), demonstrating "how the resources of the past may allow for change without wholly determining it" (466).

The novels under consideration here are not trans minor literature simply due to the subject position of their writers or characters, and their communities (both inter- and intra-textual) are not simply minoritized affinity groups, but formations extrapolating from majoritarian relational structures (amative coupling, family, labor) for minoritarian uses. Bakhtin elsewhere suggests that "New conditions enable innovations in a genre and the creation of new potentials within it, but the innovations are in no sense automatic, predetermined, or 'ready-made'" (Emerson and Morson, *Mikhail Bakhtin*, 466). Instead, works and authors react to these new conditions by entering "into a productive dialogue with available genre resources" (466). The genre resources are distinct in each site excavated in this Element, but they communicate with one another through the minoritarian, disidentifying with and disrupting generic conventions when useful, embracing them when necessary. Still we wonder, what are the epistemic wages of genre? In what ways does the assumptive scaffolding of genre allow for other flights and inventions? Put more broadly (and bluntly): Can we still be surprised by fiction, and does it matter? The reading practices I outline in this Element ought to be useful to rethink minor deterritorializations of generic categories. It is, for example, one thing to read *Detransition, Baby* *as* a family novel, another to read it *against* the history and dictates of the family novel genre, and a third to read it *through* the family novel, a disidentificatory circuitry that troubles definition of the family and how (and for whom) it can be narrativized. In this instance, the genre resources of the family novel offer cultural legibility but also opportunities to remake the very concept of family and the minoritarian stories we tell about it.

Trans Minor Genre

> "The genres of trans living are whittled down to just a few: hero worship, demonology, victimology."
>
> (Malatino, *Side Affects*, 1)

How can a structured category be anything other than normativizing? The minor answer: through strategies of disidentification and deterritorialization. Malatino theorizes a leveling of ways of representing trans living, but this leveling is perspectival, dependent upon having access to majoritarian tools of censure, exscription, and marginalization. For any one set of majoritarian tools, there can be a correspondent category of resistance strategies and technologies; trans minor literature deploys counter-normative, political, communitarian genres of resistance. Thomas Beebee (*The Ideology of Genre*) speculates on the quality of generic opposition, suggesting that "to say a work's genre is to say what it is not" (263). There are both negative (what it is not) and positive components to generic definition, but the minoritized is prepossessed of the former. To embody the subject position of "trans" is to be deemed "not cis," to be "of color" is to be "nonwhite," similarly to be disabled, to be cash poor, to be migrant, et al. But these are not genres of being, at least not in the same way I use the concept here. Instead, it is through capacities as political actors, community members, and narrative builders that the minoritized can harness genres of the minor. Beebee continues, "whether through opposition or through recursivity, genre is shown to be what it is not. Not genre so much as generic instability now offers itself as the key to understanding the text. The question now becomes, what is it that we are reading when we read generic instability?" (268). We might be reading the minor, if we are reading for generic destabilizations, the precarity of generic categories and the elements most useful to minoritarian expression.

Leslie Feinberg (*Stone Butch Blues*) returned to *Stone Butch Blues* on the occasion of its tenth anniversary, in 2003, wondering where ze would find the work in a library or a bookstore: "Which category was it in?" (309). Ze ruminates on being asked if it is a work of fiction, and is it real; Feinberg is agnostic toward the former, and as to the latter thinks "Oh, it's real all right . . . never underestimate the power of fiction to tell the truth" (309). The minor novel destabilizes the categories of memoir and fiction, truth-telling and real-ness. Juliet Jacques ("Variations") reflects not dissimilarly on the faculty of minor fiction, in the notes to the thesis form of her poly-generic collection *Variations*: "Having struggled with the burden of representing (or, at least, not misrepresenting) the trans community as a journalist and memoirist," she writes, "I felt fiction may allow me to represent that community in more playful and pluralist ways, raising questions rather than trying to answer them, and allowing me to creatively explore the relationship between literary forms and gender identities" (19–20). This relationship can be conceived of as generic contact and an associated set of reading practices, thinking of gender identities and the stories we tell and to which we commit ourselves as subject to both the normativities and genre instabilities inherent to the stuff of narrative. This body of minor literature, arguably beginning with Feinberg's first novel in 1993, to Binnie's in 2013, and to Peters's in 2021, has more than begun to explore Stone's "set of texts." Thinking, with Stone, of trans as not only a genre but a constellation of embodied texts is radical without lapsing into pure metaphor: Bodies are written and read, rendered more or less legible according to sex–gender presentation and embodiment, and, indeed, correspondence to and troubling of generic convention. When Stryker ("Frankenstein") avers that transgender rage "emerges from the interstices of discursive practices and at the collapse of generic categories" (252), she invokes an affective technology that results from the destabilization of genre.

Trans Minor Genre Reading

TransGenre wonders, with Trish Salah ("Transgender and Transgenre Writing"), about "this new minor literature, its normative conventions, and its constitutive exclusions" (174). I share Salah's commitment to "trans genre writing as minor literature, rather than an emergent, minority literature" as a means of resisting either being inscribed as a selective tradition "parallel to the hegemonic" or else a "total reconfiguration" of a selective hegemonic tradition (179). The minor describes tactics of resistance to balkanization or assimilation in order to become legible to the majoritarian. I do not necessarily account for this minor literature as "genre literature," except in the broadest sense that these novels draw promiscu- ously and strategically from a variety of generic conventions to convey both the limitations and the fluidity of said forms. Genre is transmitted through the ways in which minoritized characters account for the often phobic majoritarian, in this case, trans characters and the institutions and actors that serve to codify, amplify, or otherwise deploy their status as trans. In this way, genre becomes a means of formal identity formation, as well as a backdrop against which subaltern narrative can be understood.

Salah suggests that "if trans genre texts are subalternated, they cannot simply ask for inclusion but rather need to rearticulate the human through the literary," and that "language itself is transformed where the literary reconstitutes or refuses the terms of the human" (181). This reconstitution or refusal can be understood as a means of apprehending transness as minor genre, as Stone suggested years ago. The fungibility, the transness of genre is key to minor genre readings of this literature. Grace Lavery (*Pleasure and Efficacy*) notes the coextensive nature of terms: "Since transition, by design, takes people out of one genre and deposits them in another, it is no surprise that a cultural history of gender transition will also provide, by accident, a history of genre transition" (xii). The readings in this Element attempt to justify both the suturing and twin capitalization of its title: terms that are distinct yet circuited together into a minoritarian hermeneutic of deterritorialization.

So, what can be accomplished with trans minor genre reading practices? Structural and thematic conventions need not be normativizing by default if they are wielded through a minoritarian politics and epistemology. Over the following sections, I attempt a rethinking of genre through genre readings of constitutive categories, practices, and politics outlined at four distinct but interpenetrated sites. In so doing, I seek to activate the transgeneric as a set of resistant reading practices, not seeking to define trans from the perspective of or in contradistinction to cis, but understanding genre deterritorialization, reworking, and transgression as elemental to a radical politics of self-determination. I select these four generic sites in part due to their pronounced expression in this trans minor literature; in part for their seeming unlikeness, which renders the connections between them more marked; and in part for reasons specific to each that I will briefly detail here and expand upon in the readings themselves.

In the next section, the minor road novel offers a politics of simultaneous retreat and self-determination: setting a path and breaking it, championing irresponsibility to phobic publics and their institutions and deep commitments to discovering, unsettling, and reorienting one's sense of self. The underpinnings of class privilege and freedom of movement to travel in the absence of task or destination is ripe for deterritorialization and challenge. At the second site, what I've termed the minor mourning novel refuses necropolitics through aestheticizing grief: not memorialization and monumentality for public consumption, but preservation for minor memory and individual assimilation. Whereas the road novel uses transportation and distance to mark its generic arc, the mourning novel not wholly dissimilarly tracks the paths of affective response to loss. At the penultimate site, the minor chosen family novel suggests a politics of nuclear (family) disarmament, eliding and resisting state intervention into structures of care. Here, queer sociality presses against and masquerades as institutionally prescribed biological family kinship. Finally, the minor archival novel instigates a horizontal politics: history as a tool for reevaluation of the present, a revolutionary epistemology. I see the archival novel as a kind of reaction to the forms of the historical novel, and a way of cataloging strange and minor uses of genre more generally. Being "ahead of one's time" applies only to the majoritarian subject; the minoritarian revolutionaries are for the future but of their time – they define their time. Genre is a lens that can help reveal them.

2 The Road Novel

> "I'd been driving for such a long time, and the idea that I didn't have to do it for once was one of the most romantic things I'd heard."
>
> (*Summer Fun*, 190)

Minor Discontents of the Road Novel

There may be no such thing as a minor road novel. Not every genre needs to be recuperated, and while minor readings may be a fruitful mode of inquiry, could certain genres be so enmeshed in the majoritarian (including its countercultures) that they rely upon its conventions for their very definition? The road novel could be defined so broadly as to include minor examples, or so narrowly as to be defined by one novel only. In the first case, simply featuring "a road" in a literal and/or figurative sense would include a wide variety of fiction that does not sufficiently exhibit the kinship of genre; people take long trips in all sorts of novels. In the latter case, Jack Kerouac's *On the Road* is perhaps the signal work of the genre in the US, both formally and contextually of and defining its moment: America, jazz, Beats, postwar manifest destiny and entropic malaise in equal measure. In one sense, any subsequent narrative containing a series of meandering road trips will be compared to it; in another, it is a narrative that could be rewritten endlessly with different encounters, contexts, and other variables. In any reading, though, Kerouac's model for the road novel is young, white, working/middle class, "healthy," cis men ambling across the country, running from straight/square society, searching for . . . something.

Nevertheless, it may be simpler to define what this inquiry means by "road novel" by taking up Beebee's gambit and first considering what it is not: the road itself is insufficient as a generic marker. Further, the road novel is not a quest novel. It is important that the trip itself is a character subject to its own whims and not defined by its ostensible origin or telos. Neither is it a travel novel wherein the scenery and ports of call are the foci: descriptions of landscapes, accents, dialects, customs, and ethnography may occur along the way, but they do not themselves constitute a road novel. *The Odyssey*, *Canterbury Tales*, *Pilgrim's Progress*, and *Gulliver's Travels* all skirt along the genre as earlier instances of narrative journeys, though the means of conveyance and how directed the travels are render them significantly different. *Oliver Twist* (with its "parish boy's progress" subtitle), *Jude the Obscure*, and *Their Eyes Were Watching God* are all heavily reliant on trips and travel without necessarily falling into the quest or travel narrative category, but are still somewhat limited in the imagination of their geographies. Their trips are purposeful and even desperate, not "for their own sake." As such, the advent of the more readily available automobile feels central to the road novel – one could take to the road without "traveling" or "vacationing" in senses that required access to leisure time and expendable resources.

The generic resources of the road novel include any destination being amorphous, subject to change, or disproportionately unimportant in comparison with the journey itself. There is usually a beginning, always a middle, and only sometimes an end, which tends not to be an actual resolution. Each element of this chrono-normative structure reveals both the possibility and the friction of a minor road novel. The road novel begins with disaffection and/or a desire to remove oneself from society, either of which takes on a different register in the minor. The disaffection tends to result from a lack or spoilage of community, the failure to find or maintain territory for oneself. The removal is almost redundant for minoritized subjects: deterritorialization is necessarily a dynamic of separation and reformation, of both subject and object. The road novel could also proceed from some kind of mission (in *On the Road*, it might be to rejoin one's estranged wife or move some furniture) or necessity, but even these tend to reflect a level of privilege. Put simply, the minoritized subject does not always have the luxury to leave.

The long middle-of-the-road novel is its core, as its characters tend to exist on and for the road. As Sal notes of his traveling companion and North Star at the onset of *On the Road*, "Dean is the perfect guy for the road" (1). Minor subjects are never the perfect guy for the road, at least not from the perspective of phobic publics and their institutions. This middle tends to be all about the people and events one encounters on the road, along with various "side quests" or discovering one or more purposes en route. In the case of a potential trans minor road novel, as with each of these genres, experiences and the tropes that contain them are conditioned by subject position. Is transition itself a road, with or without a fully formed or conceived end? Are minor identity and embodiment paths toward/through … toleration, acceptance, assimilation, de-minoritization? These may be what the minor subject actually wants to depart from.

Due in part to the unclarity of the destination, the road novel, and particularly the minor road novel, is uniquely unmoored from the responsibility of a resolved end. Does the road require an end; does the end require a road; does the novel require either? In a literal sense, all novels end, and, resolved or not, the end of the road novel should be considered in this light. The sons of Christian do not cross the river at the end of *Pilgrim's Progress*, Gulliver returns home wholly dissatisfied and disidentified with human society in Swift, Jude visits Sue one final time before perishing in Hardy's novel; none of these protagonists exactly accomplish "what they set out to." Deleuze and Guattari note the "dream" of genre: to assume a major function in language. But here we might consider all of the potentially more radical aspirations of the minor: equal economic opportunity across sex–gender identities? Access to reproductive health care? Equal protection under the law? Or perhaps more intersectional, extra-legislative goals, such as the dismantling of white supremacy, or the end of capitalism, the prison industrial complex, or national borders? The major function of minor language and genre can be as radical as the deterritorialization of form and content.

To wheel back to the road novel, how white, straight, able, and masc is the road trip? As prime exemplars of the form in the twentieth century, *On the Road* and *Fear and Loathing in Las Vegas* are mostly all three of those things (though

Doctor Gonzo in Thompsons's novel is based on Oscar Acosta Fierro, a Chicano rights activist). Each novel is also a roman à clef, autofictional (to use a term coined after the publication of either) work, and easily characterized as picaresque besides. The cisnormativities of these generic designations are based in part on their prerequisite privilege of access and freedom of movement: these novels are not about to have their protagonists repeatedly harassed by the law, unless as a device to outwit it, escape it, or wield it as a device for some other ends. And so the questions of the road novel are more "why" than "what," taking some of the emphasis off of causally justified succession of narrative events and putting it onto character motivations and how they react to given scenarios and stimuli. *On the Road* features a class of characters who operate through largely white, working-/educated-class masculinity as they move impecuniously across a big country, sensing they will always be okay in the end. A minoritarian road novel does not feature this luxury for its characters: their ostensible reasons for being on the road tend to be clearer and a bit more urgent, and the characters and scenarios they encounter always carry with them the threat of phobic publics or the promise of minoritarian community.

Half a Road to Nevada

Binnie's *Nevada* is the alpha and omega of the trans minor road novel; it warrants analysis due to its influence, relative earliness, and sense of how much has/has not changed in the decade since its initial publication. For this first genre site, I will focus on this seminal work, noting some others that deploy road novel genre resources afterward. Maria's journey in *Nevada* is just as easily decontextualized as Sal and Dean's (though it is crucial that there are two of them, as well as a host of characters who join them along the way, whereas Maria is profoundly alone until stopping), but the history Maria carries is not the history of a nation, a generation, 'angry young men,' etcetera. The novel is not premised on if Maria is a "good" person; she has persisted and can tell little Maria and all the other little Marias a story of not just survival, but fulfillment of a desired variety of embodiment. There is obviously a certain privilege to much of her movement, but that's almost beside the point, for better or for worse. *Nevada* is half of a road novel and traces a map of minoritarian subjectivity in transcontinental isolation.

Early on in the novel, Maria thinks back on her hometown in Pennsylvania: "Kids in patch pants sit out in front of the coffee shoppe on main street talking about how they're going to get out, how they're going to start a band or write like Kerouac and go on tour and move to the city" (16). We know already that Maria has gotten out, does not write like Kerouac (though "reads so much that she assumes one day she'll have an idea and put together a Great Anti-American Novel or two" [95]), but has moved to New York City and is a writer, even if she might not identify primarily as such. She has fulfilled the bulk of her ilk's exurban expatriate orientation. By the time the road novel element of *Nevada* begins to crest, Maria has blown apart her life and provisions herself with enough heroin (if not any professed intention) to kill herself, and texts her now former girlfriend, Steph, to borrow her car for "a couple of days," to which the beleaguered ex replies with the mantra of the novel: "whatever" (133). In many senses, this is the ideal opening for a road novel: some tenuous threads back to wherever one has left, and only the foggiest sense of where one is going (because that is not the important thing). "She drives into Manhattan over the bridge she's ridden her bike over every morning for the last six years," (133), and as she does, "Fuck this, she thinks. Fuck this city. Fuck this coast. What if I just go to fuckin California or something" (133). But the title of the novel makes plain what the reader might guess from reading its first half: she will stop at "or something" before she makes "fuckin California."

The first half of *Nevada* could be read through a number of generic lenses: relationship/breakup novel, woman-in-the-city/urban novel, trans auto-ethnography… we could generate a few more that presage some of the trans minor literature that has followed in this novel's wake. In this first half, Maria acknowledges her successes, somewhat: she has found some community, her first amative relationship as a woman, work, the (desired) ability to pass more often than not, a sense of what her body needs. But she found nothing not worth leaving behind, including her beloved bike, which she devastatingly tells Steph during their apparent breakup is "the only way I know to really be in touch with my life, with the world outside myself" (72). This equivocation represents both the suture of *Nevada* and the splitting open of the road novel form: traveling alone (as one generally must by bicycle) is both Maria's sole conveyance to be in touch with her life (epistemology), and her knowing the outside world (phenomenology). The road novel tends to render judgment of its travelers strictly through how they interact with encounters on the road – they are strangers in strange lands and must apprehend and adjudicate customs and sensibilities. Maria claims to know herself and her world only from the seat of her bicycle, and so taking to the automobile becomes a literally and figuratively accelerated version of the same. This way of knowing bears on one's sense of time (punctuated and measured against "stops" along the way) and identity (Maria will present herself [or not] to a spectrum of America far from the safety of hipster Williamsburg or anonymous Manhattan).

But the experiment of the road novel half of the work relegates Maria to the background and consequently leaves the reader to wonder about the 2,500 miles that separate her from the subject of the first seven chapters of the novel's second part, James. This is not expected road novel stuff, and each detail we read about James refracts through Maria's impending arrival. James, not unlike Maria, hates lots of things, and is particularly troubled by the morass of his relationship with Nicole, his nascent desire to wear women's clothes, and the frustrated impulses to web search sissy porn and autogynephilia that he can understand only as scrambled erotic needs. Whereas he seeks rationalizations ("He wasn't transsexual. He just wanted dresses" [155]), Maria arrives in Star City, Nevada, with convictions: "That kid is trans and he doesn't even know it yet" (162). For his part, James is "working on it" (140) as he awaits Maria's arrival, thinking about being trans "all the fucking time" but "can't imagine actually being trans in the real world" (171). Everything happens for a reason in fiction – there is always an author selecting details for inclusion – and even in the case of the road novel there cannot truly be a "chance encounter." Nevertheless, Binnie telegraphs this meeting far more than one might expect in an uncanny travelogue full of apparently happenstantial meetings and events "along the way." Just as Maria clocks James, so too does James read Maria as trans, wondering, "How could I tell? It was probably some kind of combination of things," and, equally pressingly, "Could other people tell?" (169–170). Fated though it may seem, nearly every aspect of Maria and James's encounter is frustrated; she is a comet of late-stage transition crashing into his deep agnosticism around sexuality and sex–gender. The trans minor road novel dispenses with the actual road in favor of the encounter, the possibility of community, the moments of anonymous care and longing, even though they are ultimately frustrated. It deterritorializes the form of the chance encounter onto the life-saving, community-building, fated meeting, which ultimately (or at least immediately) fails.

Thus we're only granted glimpses of Maria's road narrative in retrospect: she notes how she hasn't talked to anyone, has taken her time moving westward, worn the same clothes repeatedly … there would be nothing to narrate save for her own thoughts, which would not really fit the morphology of a road novel. Furthermore, Maria does find purpose in Star City and retrofits the trip to it. As she considers going back into Walmart to see the encounter through with James, she decides: "This is what's going on, Maria, this is what you're doing, this is the whole point of this trip you're on right now. This thing. Right here" (174). In the midst of her irresponsibility tour – a road novel trope if ever there was one – Maria has found someone for whom to be responsible. And this responsibility is based on expertise, which is also central to the road novel (as well as the picaresque; the rogue must have their wits, strength, and/or guile about them): "The central thing here is that Maria is really good at being trans" (174). This is not a realization at the end of the novel; it is a frictive theme throughout. To paraphrase Sal's depiction of Dean, Maria is the "perfect femme" for this task. Steph thinks, "Sometimes it seems like being trans is the only bad thing that has ever really happened to Maria" (121), but that's not quite fair, even if Maria's behavior and affect precipitate some of the other bad things. Road novel characters – from Tom Jones to Huck Finn to Raoul Duke – are good at being on the road. Maria is good at thinking about being good at being trans. Though "Maria can explain to you exactly what she's figured out and how she figured it out and can smell cisnormativity from like a hundred yards," it remains the case that "she just sucks at pretty much everything else" (175). To excel at being on the road perhaps precludes finding its terminus.

Nevada's eschewal of responsibility can easily be read as road novel privilege, but there's no privilege in casting oneself out of a society designed to make one ill-fit. It's only a matter of how one does it, or what means or models one is presented to do so. The meeting with James is going to frustrate them both, as he discerns when Maria passes out after they eat frozen food in his apartment: "This is probably James's first clue that this girl isn't going to give him the adventure in personal growth, or at least the cool story, that he was hoping for" (187). This is the aborted promise of the road, and what separates it from *Bildungsroman*. Maria's pitch, however, is successful, asking James "Do I want to have the kind of life where I call out of work to go to Reno with a cool wingnut stranger lady, or do I want to have the kind of life where I work loyally for Walmart until I die?" (202). The road novel is conditioned by shaking off pattern and inevitably reproducing it, mistaking lack of control over whom you meet with taking control over your own behavior and narrative. As Maria loses control of the narrative of James's latent transness, the illusion of their familiarity or closeness is shattered; there exists no default community, no t4egg or t4(possibly)t here. She ends up drifting out of the narrative for the closing chapters, left in a casino with James having stolen half of her heroin and waiting to be picked by Nicole.

The deterritorializations here are many, but the road as a place for perfunctory relationships, hangers-on and those left behind, revelations great and small is simply mooted. There is no robust community to be founded on cyclically running away any more than one strictly based on making the best of a bad situation, even if harm reduction and separation can both be elements of radical minoritarian community-making. *Nevada*'s responsibilities are to a rather unflinching unwillingness to allow its minor protagonist a discreet moral victory; instead, the road is laid bare for what it is: promising nothing and unlikely to offer the sought-after "why."

Other Trans Minor Roads

There are, of course, trans minor novels that include some variety of "why" without lapsing fully into quest novels. Joss Lake's *Future Feeling* sends its trans protagonists to rescue another trans subject at the behest of a technofuturistic mutual aid organization. But how Pen and Aiden are to go about rescuing Blithe is exceedingly loose, and the choices they make regarding how to best go about it are their own. This is a road novel with an externally mandated t4t ethic, in which the travelers are not escaping or questing toward anything, but rather laboring to help another who shares their minoritized subject position to escape. RE Katz's *And then the Gray Heaven* similarly has a recognizable purpose for its travels – to memorialize a dead lover – but again decides on the details of the goal only as the novel progresses. Jules will bury portions of B's ashes, but there is no telos for queer grief, as examined further in *TransGenre*'s inquiry into what I term the mourning novel. But despite *Gray Heaven*'s rather distant travels, the actual mechanics of moving across the country are essentially written out of the narrative – it refuses to become a road novel. In another register, Jeanne Thornton's *Summer Fun* teeters on the brink of a road novel, baiting the reader into considering what sort of story would spin out from the protagonist, Gala, actually running off with interloper Caroline to find the latter's grandmother, who ghost cowrote many of Gala's idol's hit songs in the 1960s. This last instance is instructive of the balance of privilege, irresponsibility, and becoming in a trans minor (aborted) road novel. Whereas *Nevada* has its protagonist occupy the protracted narrative center of being "on the road," *Summer Fun* dares its youngish, somewhat disaffected, bad-job-with-no-prospects-having star to run away from it all, and she does not. Gala has an acute sense of her tether to work, community with trans femme friend Ronda, and access to gender-affirming health care. Charity Porpentine Heartscape's *Serious Weakness* offers another deformation of the road novel as abduction novel, its sociopathic antagonist Insul force-feminizing and annihilating the subject-hood of Trianon/Tria throughout its increasingly brutalist episodes. Porpentine experiments with hundreds of pages of body horror crescendo as the road becomes the entirety of both Insul's and Tria/non's identities, forging a grotesque kind of enforced community and mutual dependence between them.

The Trans Minor Road Novel

Do these instances offer prospects for a trans minor road novel, or simply its foreclosure? Can the minoritarian be enacted on the road, or are the strategies for contending with the road simply those of survival and getting back off of it?

The road is neither a purpose nor a telos for these protagonists; if anything, it simply creates (literal and figurative) distance with their presents. Maria's past is already set at some level of remove as trans subjects, which is the case for most of the major trans characters in this body of literature. The road is instead a conduit for aesthetic and amative closure, deterritorializing the aimless, latent energies of the road novel form and reappropriating them onto trans (-gressive, -continental, -versal) desire. The prospect for a trans minor road novel is in part disavowing – it offers instead a minor revaluation of abandonment, appraisal, and remapping as one passes the lonesome miles. In each of these cases, the travelers are compelled, however, through community or lack thereof. Maria's victory is in part the ability to fly solo, and even that is stunted when she runs into James. These novels trouble any singular or final sense of ends, and their resolutions are by and large left to the reader's assumption or design. To be irresponsible, to mourn, to ameliorate harm, to survive and create some measure of comfort or safety are the exits from the road novel form, and serve to undercut the romance of "finding oneself" in the anonymity of other travelers.

And so the trans minor road novel thematizes duration in a way that reflects Atalia Israeli-Nevo's sense of "taking time" as a modality of trans temporality: "a way of thinking and experiencing life and body through delay and untimeliness" (42). Israeli-Nevo herself notes the ways in which Maria's lack of fastidiousness with her hormone injections in *Nevada* forces her into "takin time with her transition" (42), but the road novel half of the work is no less centered on this anti-chrono-normative sense of timing. The trans road novel (and, as it happens, each of the genres in this Element) is predicated on an economy of time that is out of step with the normativities of fiction, and thus the seeming lack of resolved ending can be understood as another symptom of time being taken.

3 The Mourning Novel

"Your friends will do their best to comfort you
Your friends will set their favorite traps for you
At night they'll worry in their beds about you
At night the moon will come and sing for you
At last, you'll have something you can call the world."
(Roselit Bone, "Ofrenda")

Who Mourns the Unmournable, and How

Mourning is where loss is taken up by affect; the human capacity to mourn is made legible commensurate with the capacity to experience and fathom loss and in some way respond. This capacity and these responses carry with them a third, more communitarian component of responsibility to oneself, to the object of mourning, and to the community between them and beyond. A minoritarian sense of mourning values the last of these as a means to expand upon and re/imagine the first two. Ginetta E. B. Candelario ("Editor's Introduction") suggests that "feminist mourning politicizes and historicizes the disproportionately high impact and negative experience of loss of life has on those who belong to vulnerable communities, identities, and social statuses" (300). A minoritarian politicization and historicization also carves out space for imagination, radical horizontal thinking not simply ensuring loss not being "in vain" for community memory, but for mourning to have value in itself. The narrativization of minoritarian mourning can express the aporia of at once living outside of majoritarian time (expressed through politics and history) and at the same time experiencing its dictates and mortal terminus. Thus, the trans minor mourning novel "takes time" to reconstruct the relationship between absence and persistence within and across minoritarian community. Death and loss may come to us all, but their stories – who writes, reads, and understands them – are not at all the same.

Novels tend to be structured from the ending, in that they are bounded by a minimum (and maximum?) duration, resolving in some manner the plot and characters. They are, in this sense, always more about the journey than the destination. Mourning is itself all about the pivot or the gulf between ending and beginning. To be "in mourning" means something/someone has died and one has not "gotten over it" such that the affective resonance remains sufficiently encompassing to bear remark. This gerundial form, "in mourning," is ideal material for long-form fiction, as it appears to imply a before-during-after structure that can be mimetically understood by a wide variety of readership and reference to both one's own and broader cultural experiences. This is perhaps true of genre in general: Its morphology is contoured not by verisimilitude, but by the extent to which a reader can rely on cultural and experiential norms – what Jameson termed in "Magical Narrative" "proper use of cultural artifacts" – to evaluate a given generic structure. Mourning, then, is not a necessary component of loss, but loss (or at least the perception thereof) is prerequisite for mourning. To the extent that novels are character-driven, they are also development-driven, and development means gain and loss, persistence and acquiescence. This loss does not necessarily have to be death, but mourning seems most poignant and impactful when its object cannot return or respond. Communitarian mourning is so vital for minoritized subjects in part due to this lack of return/answer; when one's communities of feeling are potentially so small to begin with, and when the grievability of their lives is in such question (at least for majoritarian publics), a single loss becomes all the more profound.

And so death is a cord running through trans minor literature. Reese in *Detransition, Baby* muses on attending trans women's funerals; Kai Cheng Thom's "Lipstick Lacerators" mourn the death of the "first femme," among others in the City of Smoke in *Fierce Femmes and Notorious Liars*; Joshua Whitehead's titular *Jonny Appleseed* works their way to their kokum's funeral throughout the arc of the novel; Paul's beloved Tony Pinto's death from AIDS-related complications bubbles up throughout Andrea Lawlor's *Paul Takes the Form of a Mortal Girl*; Wendy is thrown into alcoholic despair at the loss of her trans sister Sophie in the course of Casey Plett's *Little Fish*. But none of these is a mourning novel, per se, no matter how suffused with losses both potential and realized they may be. Impactful as the deaths both named and anonymous are throughout their narratives, they do not structure the novels in such a way that they are "about" the loss and subsequent mourning. The three novels on which this section focuses very much are, such that mourning is omnipresent and inflects the affective, embodied, identitarian, and narrative/plot elements of the works. This section builds toward a genre reading of trans minor mourning novels by mapping out narratives of mourning more broadly, then narrowing to minoritarian/minoritized mourning, and finally theorizing minor communitarian mourning as a narrative practice, reading loss into life.

Mourning

Before considering the trans minor mourning novel, a broad-strokes sketch of generic conventions and genre resources of mourning in narrative is needed. There must first be an affective bond whose absence will be more or less acutely felt. When we consider minor literature, this affective bond can be more diffuse, in the sense that the loss of any member of minoritarian community "hits differently" and inflects the experiences of those who remain. Relatedly, there must be death and/or loss with some sense of irrevocability or immutability. It significantly changes the stakes and narrative arc to include some possibility of return, excepting the sense in which memorial itself is a kind of persistence. This is to say, for example, the titular Little Blue Encyclopedia of Plante's novel retains Vivian's presence in its way, but there is no metaphysical sense in which she will return from the dead. Next, the mourning novel must concern itself with suffering, grief, and/or melancholy, the inward or outward expressions of and reactions to said loss(es). Mourning becomes legible only though methods, tactics, and strategies of reaction and amelioration. Furthermore, these strategies are rarely as simple as "feeling better" or "moving on," but through their narrativization account for the meaning (or lack thereof) of the object of loss and relationship thereto. In the novel, this tends to mean considering this object/

relationship before the loss, during the mourning, and after the resolution of mourning, if it exists; thus, a tripartite chronology of mourning emerges.

Minor Mourning

So as we turn to minor mourning, it is worth noting: This is not meant to be the "trans death novel" section, as that would not be a genre in the same sense this Element deploys. As much as mourning is about the object, the novel is more proficient as a subjectifying machine, and so the mourning novel is more about minor subjects than minor objects. There is also a self-reflexivity to minor mourning that renders it both communitarian and individual at once. As Awkward-Rich (*The Terrible We*) asks, "What becomes of the object after it has survived its own loss?" (146); the minoritized subject survives their own loss at each instance of the loss of part of their communities. Minor mourning prompts a variety of other, specific questions, the first being what does it mean for life to be grievable, or not? Butler (*Precarious Life*) considers this question in terms of geopolitics, noting the ways in which "Certain lives will be highly protected, and the abrogation of their claims to sanctity will be sufficient to mobilize the forces of war. Other lives will not find such fast and furious support and will not even qualify as 'grievable'" (32). While mourning may not, in itself, alter the broader political order, it can transform individual and communitarian relations. Butler writes of mourning as "submitting to a transformation" the results of which "one cannot know in advance" (21), but which ultimately "furnishes a sense of political community of a complex order" (22). The minor novel is an ideal laboratory for this complex order, taking up the cause of both speculating on and renarrativizing relationships in loss. Butler notes that, in grief, "I tell a story about the relations I choose, only to expose, somewhere along the way, the way I am gripped and undone by these very relations. My narrative falters, as it must" (23). The novel can resist, exploit, or embrace this faltering.

Furthermore, mourning brings about new, subverted, forgotten, or lost counter/narratives regarding subjects who can reemerge only through literal or affective archives, some of which are never meant to be discovered. Wendy mourns both her grandfather's lost queerness and Sophie in *Little Fish*; Jules has to contend with B's art practice, family, and queerness in retrospect in *Gray Heaven*; Zelda thinks around Viv's "darker" past in *Little Blue*; Reese mourns the physical limitations on her carrying a child, then the loss of one to a potential abortion in *Detransition, Baby*. Each of the novels under consideration are archives of loss and becoming; minor subjects are not afforded space to mourn other minor subjects, and this body of literature is thus a deterritorialization of grief and a series of reterritorializations through Hirsch's "conventionalized predictions or guesses." They thematize trans mourning in the persistence of minoritarian community and the diffusion of loss across minor subjectivity.

Minor Mourning via Object/ification

Each generic mutation and deterritorialization carries with it not just thematically distinct, but structurally and perspectively varied questions and challenges. In the case of the road novel, trans minor literature questions the motivations, experiences, and purposes of its subjects. Characters move through space in ways that underscore the privilege of being able to "turn on, tune in, drop out" and entropically meander against societal convention. Trans characters in these novels take their time on the road because they have different relationships to both pastness and futurity, expressed in this minor fiction through non-teleological narrative structures and refusal of answers to causal "why" questions regarding motivation. The mourning novel adds a clearer sense of subject–object relationships; even the most diffuse, generalized, or aestheticized sense of grief must have an object. Plante's *Little Blue Encyclopedia (for Vivian)* reflects the ways in which minor mourning fails to progress through stages, instead moving along axes that implicate relationships between community, embodied grief, and nonlinear alteration/mutation/renarrativization. Tracking these axes in *Little Blue* – a novel chronicling its narrator's mourning of the recently deceased Vivian – provides some scaffolding for the minoritarian deterritorializations of the other novels.

The titular encyclopedia is what holds the novel together structurally; the narrator (unnamed until the "Z" entry is reached, as Vivian endorses her choice of "Zelda" for a new moniker) works through the alphabet according to the characters of the fabulated, short-lived television program *Little Blue*. The majoritarian, progressivist presumption might be that documenting her beloved lost friend and trans mentor of sorts would be part of an effort to memorialize (that is, allow Vivian to "live on" through the book), ameliorate (lessen the pain in some way), and/or progress ("move on" and continue her own life); various characters urge the narrator to do precisely those things. Her own designs shift and transform and are never entirely clear to begin with, but she keeps a to-do list on a sticky note on her laptop, including "Turn pain into beauty" (156). It is a depersonalized imperative, and she notes, "It seemed as elusive as turning lead into gold," but the impetus is at least in part, "Viv had done it" (156). Viv had done it with her friendship, not by offering a model of trans woman-ness, but an affective community for the narrator to join. While the trans minor road novel is marked by unexpected sources of minoritarian community on the road, the mourning novel in some senses thematizes community anticipating, through, and after death. To attempt to turn "the pain of losing Viv into a weepy and witty alphabetical elegy" is an effort at transformation into beauty even if (or perhaps by dint of) "it hasn't really made me feel alphabetter" (156). It has not, and it will not. Feeling better as the telos of mourning elides the communitarian loss that cannot be restored. As the narrator puts it later in the novel, memory is insufficient, in part because it often sustains the death itself. She notes that "Trans women of color are murdered for trying to live their lives," and there is value in simply remembering them, but not as a substitute for knowing "who they were, how they lived, who and what they loved in this world" (182–183). Minoritarian mourning is neither an excavation nor a rehabilitation; it is an outgrowth of an impossible desire to know as fully as possible who and how someone loves.

There is a personal locus of loss for the narrator as well. The novel opens by bridging the pain of loss with the desire to remain close through something beloved (in this instance, television and music). Cataloging the embodied effects of loss is a more pronounced activity for subjects who are charged with understanding and reforming their own bodies/psyches/emotions from the moment they understand themselves as not cis. The narrator writes, "When Vivian died, my world collapsed" (1); she weeps, her senses dull, "everything and everyone around me receded" (1). The affective experiences of mourning are "a sad dream" (2), "numb and stunned" (14), "emptiness and anger" (19) – nothing in and of itself all that unusual. Though the drive to record Vivian emanates in part from a desire to keep her from "disappear[ing] from this world, unremembered and unseen" (13), the narrator repeatedly notes how little of her friend's life she truly knew. It is absence that ripples through the work long before the death that drives the narrative. Rewatching *Little Blue* is hardly a palliative experience, and "writing about [Vivian] wasn't like being with her" (14). The narrator only grows "more acutely aware that she was gone, that her thoughts were gone, her words were gone, her body was gone" (14). In turn, the mourner becomes "increasingly aware" of her own "body, of all the things I had done in it and all the things I could do in it" (14). This axis of loss welds grievability to embodiment; the absence of a crucial element of the author's community prompts her to consider all that her own body may be capable of, as well as its responsibilities.

Attachment is both prerequisite for and oppositional to loss. Mourning becomes legible to the extent that attachment can be understood, but minor mourning carries with it the additional attachment of affective community and shared subject position. That said, the focus of *Little Blue* is particular, one-to-one attachments (to Viv's sister Dot, to the narrator's brother, to other mutual friends), each in comparison and contradistinction to not so much Vivian in life, but Vivian in death. The narrator "never understood why Viv gravitated towards" (2) her, but realizes in no uncertain terms how much she loved and was in love with Viv (10, 107, 176). This realization is based on a concretization of mortality, and one's own diminishment in the shadow of loss: The only affirmation seems to be the strength of the bond between the object of mourning and the subject who remains. The narrator notes how she is less ashamed than before meeting Vivian, and speculates "that one of the reasons she paid so much attention to me was that I was so shy and uncomfy in my skin" (89). She notes how she "needed Viv more than [Viv] needed me" (135), and that Viv's life "mattered to me" as well as "lots of other people" (143). The narrator encounters a few of these people throughout the narrative, but will never ascertain how their own needfulness or loss measured up to her own. Vivian is her lifeline and her community; she writes the encyclopedia in part because Vivian "was there for me at the most difficult time in my life. When nobody else was there" (175–176) and in part because "She kept me alive" (176), realizing that this glossary of an obscure television show is a funny way of doing the same. But the ubiquity of loss is a definitive element of the minor mourning novel. "Viv lost so many people when she told them she was trans" (6), and the minor is informed in part by these sorts of losses: institutional erasures, of history, family, rights, culture, body. One could argue that minor experiences of these losses is more of one "never having had," but one cannot realize fully what has been taken or barred from them until they see what used to exist, what still does for others, or what can be imagined in a better future. The narrator notes how "If you spend hundreds of hours with someone, you have a catalogue of tiny memories. As you live your life, those tiny memories snap and crackle your synapses. It can be overwhelming, like the world is already overlaid with experience" (93). The overlay of experience is how the narrator's relationship with Viv in mourning conditions their present experience of the world. *Little Blue* presents a sense of embodied memory, a persistent attachment that its narrator lives out through her experience of her beloved's favorite television program and her own sense of trans woman-ness. The overlay of mourning perpetuates what would otherwise be a loss of community and what it has given the minor subject.

Minor Mourning as Aesthetic Memorial

Jules is forced throughout *And then the Gray Heaven* to account for how they mourn B, from B's lying in a coma from which he will not recover, to trekking across the country to retrace B's professional and artistic life. Minor mourners must justify not only the grievability of whom they mourn, but their own status and comportment as mourners. Jules reflects on their being separated from B after the latter's accident: "A quiz: Q: What kind of horrible creature breaks into a hospital room and blocks the door to quietly lie on the floor. A: The creature who has been erased" (31). Jules has made room for the monster in the mourning novel genre; the un-grieve-worthy forcing their way through medical, familial, and carceral institutions to mourn the ungrievable. *Gray Heaven* works along similar axes of memory, death, loss, and attachment, and shares *Little Blue*'s sense of memorialization without immobilization. But whereas the latter's narrator mourns someone she loved as model, mentor, and romantic impossibility, Jules is most distinctly mourning a lover. In each instance, however, their closeness renders them a community of two, meaning the loss of one has a hermeneutic bearing on the other: When B dies, Jules's minoritized existence and embodiment are diffused over the whole of their suddenly solitary status.

The diffusion is dialectical, between the base of the body and the superstructure of world. Throughout their relationship and particularly in B's injury and death, Jules is repeatedly reminded (by B's family, the hospital, and the law) that they are unworthy of their attachment to and thus the loss of B. Jules justifiably marvels at the depths of their erasure from permissible mourning, wondering "What does a person do when the person they love is dying in front of them? What is the punishment for holding their hand?" (27). The conditions of Jules's mourning are thus punitive, at least to begin with, as they are prohibited from exercising their care and subsequent grief in proximity to its object. These prohibitions open onto some broader questions around grievability and mourn-worthiness: When subject positions are deemed more disposable, both their grief and their grievability are mooted. After barricading themselves in B's hospital room for as long as they can, Jules is forced to contend with the oncoming likelihood of loss (a very different position on this axis from that of *Little Blue*'s narrator). The time between loss and attachment is something like persistence; it is quite different to wonder "why am I still here" when it is less than surprising when members of one's communities are more likely to perish. Jules follows this thinking to its natural end: "It was supposed to be me. I should have been dead by now" (2), but there are never any specific reasons why. Again, grievability and grief-worthiness are diffuse in their expression – minor mourning can grieve itself through its own object.

Nonetheless, it wasn't Jules who died, and now they must contend with having a body while the other body they shared their life with is reduced to ashes. Genre is not strictly about structure; it also regards theme and affect. Mourning is a structuring device for these minor novels, but it is not strictly dictated by theme: How and why characters mourn in various ways follow patterns they cannot predict in advance, unless there is some fixed (cultural or community-based) ritual in place. The Little Blue Encyclopedia is not such a ritual, it is ad hoc and perhaps even incommensurate with the task of mourning one's closest dead relation. Similarly, B never asked to have their ashes hidden in three museums in which they labored. Jules's coconspirator, Theo, realizes the plan: "Three museums, says Theo. You want to bury B in these places they made" (87); Jules concurs: "Right, I want to bring them home" (87). While Jules repeatedly refers to the ashes as simply "B," they are under no further illusions of the persistence of the corporeal body they love(d). Instead, *Gray Heaven* supplements the axes of memory/memorialization, death, attachment, and loss with the persistent problem of embodiment and simply having a body. If minor epistemology and experience is based in appreciable part on what a given body connotes and how it is read, then minor mourning contends with the bareness of that signifier being lost. Put another way, minor mourning is steeped in listening to/for those who can no longer directly respond.

In the case of Jules and B, mourning is a conduit for dis/embodiment, prompting Jules to variously forget or rediscover their own body. In addition to "it should/could have been me who was lost," Jules speculates that, in their mourning, "I am not here." As they attempt to recount the out-of-body, superhuman experience of blocking the hospital door while giving a police report, they observe, "I stopped the tears but there was something else in me that wouldn't be stopped" (24). This something else is not a surplus (or deficit) but an alternative; Jules is in one of their "darkest moments," when "everything we say is a lie" (24); they conclude, "We just can't show up for our own version of events" (24). This presents a problem for a novel told from the first person: the only version of events we have is Jules's, but on the axis of dis/embodiment, not showing up is itself a strategy. The locus of control is important in this term – strategy – rather than its more automatized analog – mechanism. When Elisabeth Kübler-Ross refers to "coping mechanisms" in *On Death and Dying*, it is almost always in tandem with the term "defense" (112), and judged on a scale of how "radical" (34) a given mechanism is. But a mechanism is just raw machinery; it is only as radical as it is perceived to be, and the deployment and consequences of affective devices and reactions vary according to both the deployer and observers. Point being, as we have seen, minor subjects may have both limitations and exceptions placed on their mourners and mourning. The strategies of the trans mourning novel allow for bodies to be placed in the same nexus of axes with death, memory, loss, and attachment to subtle and powerful effect. It is through loss that Jules requires memory/reminding to attach them to a world that no longer includes their beloved.

This can be a sensory reminder – auditory: "I need the sound now: confirmation that I am here, material, real" (33), or haptic-affective: "I realize for the millionth time that I also have a body, and I feel a pang of humiliation followed by a hot wave of grief" (38). Jules needs a body and is humiliated/bereaved by it. They "think about how my body is my own best catastrophe snack. A dark thought. Darkest. I am my darkest self right now. Everyone else is darkest thems" (38). Mourning novels centered on death include embodiment among the genre resources, which is accented for minor subjects whose bodies are often forced out of place and time. This mourning can consume one's own body in catastrophic moments; to devour the body when the body is the only thing left. Jules approaches the mind–body problem with a Cartesian question to B (in memory): "Are you your brain or your body?" (80). The stakes of this query, recalled in the midst of Jules's mourning, are highlighted: Identity is reduced to a binary not centered (explicitly, anyway) on race, class, sex–gender, or ability, but the implicitly individual. Jules's memory continues, "B thought for a second. I wish I were my body. Me too, I said. Maybe some people are" (80). Some people, but not the darkest thems. Jules and B may or may not be their brains, but they affirm they are not their bodies either. As Jules stalks the museums, admiring the various taxidermy and model displays, they "imagine B and I are these creatures, and it is the others who do not belong here, not us. This is our museum. B and me: we're just more bodies, more dust, more objects at rest" (123). Jules is forced to imagine being creatures without corporeal, human bodies. They belong in these "cultural institutions," in the spaces from which they've been barred, because in mourning they can imagine themselves beyond corporeality. Belonging, in the sense of one's presence being endorsed, is not a primary value for the minor; deterritorialization requires reframing what belongs to minoritarian community and (lovingly, violently, or both) relocating it to relative safety. In a final moment of embodiment, Jules watches Theo leave the museum where they must wait alone to deposit B's ashes. Jules describes how "a new grief mixes with old grief in my body, and I'm out" (125) – out of body, out of belonging, out of the world. Jules considers "how there is too much world to know about that is so unconcerned with me," extending the mind–body problem into the breadth of knowability. But the solution is in the mourning itself: "I need B's good severe diamond eye – to watch for me and watch me. It took me so long to know myself, to begin living: how will I do it without them. To place just one part of my calf on just one part of their thigh again when we're sitting next to each other on the couch" (125). The desire for touch is overwhelming, it runs counter to belonging in the world. Jules experiences something similar, earlier in the novel, at the smell of B on a T-shirt: "I'm out. I don't mean that I faint, I just mean I'm out on my feet" (39). Minor mourning fiction narrativizes this "being out," this wonder at persistence, this irreplaceability of loss and the strategies to conserve any beauty therefrom.

T. Fleischmann (*Time Is the Thing a Body Moves Through*) speculates on the bodily and the ways in which it does or does not ground the subject. They write, "What a relief that is, that any touch will end. But a body absent a body is a body that cannot be set, cannot be anchored in place and subjected to the process by which we racialize, gender, assess through our senses" (54). Jules's minor mourning is at once sensationalizing, touching B's ashes, burying them in museum displays, encountering elements of B's past in the form of old friends and mentors along the way, and at the same time hidden, clandestine, infiltrative. Touch has ended; only memory and attachment through time remain. As in *Little Blue*, belonging in the world is both attenuated (by losing one to/with whom the minor subject belonged in community) and reinforced (as they are forced to move beyond "why not me" to "why any of us"). Still, though each of these novels focuses on strategies for becoming alongside those of belonging, another probes this particular axis more deeply and explicitly.

Minor Mourning as Becoming

Zeyn Joukhadar's *The Thirty Names of Night* opens with a scene of memorialized mourning, as "Tonight, five years to the day since" protagonist Nadir has lost their mother, "forty-eight white-throated sparrows fall from the sky" (1). Nadir is alone in the metaphysical, "the divine was nowhere to be found," and the dead swallows "are my only companions in grief, the omen that keeps" (1) them from leaping off their grandmother's apartment building. Nadir's transition narrative is essentially in parallel with their extended mourning, watching their grandmother age, enduring attacks both literal and figurative on their Arab community in New York City. But this mourning novel is more longitudinal or generational, involving a "lost" species of bird that only Nadir's mother and a couple of other people believe actually existed. The bird becomes talismanic, linking Nadir to a history of queerness and transness that is reflected in part of their tight social circle and the lost queer history of Arab migrant artist Laila Z. As such, five years later, Nadir's mother is more an emblem of loss and an even stronger, more immediate presence than Vivian or B: Nadir is routinely in the room with her ghostly specter, displacing mourning onto other objects, not least of which, again, is Nadir's own body.

In these minor narratives, mourning the body can be an impetus for change, a desire to comfort one's younger self that there is a path through, and a sometimes-embattled celebration of finding any path to actualization or realization at all. *Little Blue*'s narrator and Jules are realized in their sex–gender and desire in large part through the relationships with the lovers they mourn. Heteronormative tropes of one's "better half" or being somehow completed by the object of desire do not hold – the mourning is the retention of the other and their addition into the architecture of the self. Nadir is highly aware of their mourn-worthy body, from the gynecologist's office in which they wish "there were another way to exist in the world than to be bodied" (3), to meeting with "male classmates from art school," who console Nadir that "few of the girls we studied with were painting anymore" (5). Nadir reflects, "It is one thing to have a body; it is another thing to struggle under the menacing weight of its meaning" (5). The reminders of having a body are entirely sex-gendered: the presence of breasts and the twinge of a binder prompt Nadir to blot out their chest with black paint in a self-portrait (44), to dissociate from their body during a strenuous basketball game (125), and to cover their belly with black pen decorations when they feel "like my body isn't mine" (60). At the Y, in a gendered changing room, they "suppress the urge to scream," go "limp with resignation," and finally "walk to the mirror to convince myself that I am here, in this body" (60). To mourn another, to be pressed with the fragility of the body and the seeming permanence of its expiration, suggests another kind of mourning and tentative acceptance. Until Nadir becomes Nadir (and with artifacts thereafter), the "constant wish" is to "exist outside myself, that I could disappear the wrongness in me" (61). Each of the axes of mourning enfold minor embodiment: reflecting on, experiencing, and acting upon existence as a marked and discomfited body, one inconvenient to and prohibited by phobic publics.

The crucial distinction here is between mourning one's body (coded as identity formation and/or perspective) and mourning within a body, a difference drawn through troubling identity and the impetus of becoming. When Nadir's bio-sister Reem is forced to confront Nadir's embodied truth, the younger sibling shakes as they make clear "I'm not a woman" (174). Reem understands, with a caveat: "I know what it's like to want something people think is wrong … But I have to mourn my sister" (174). It is an ugly note, and Nadir feels a "knot of shame" at "being mourned as though I am dead" (174). But mourning drives the broader narrative not because trans characters are presented as more adept at or experienced with it (though there could be reasons for both), but because the transition narrative itself questions grievability and persistence through loss. Nadir "learned a long time ago that things that happened years ago never really go away"; instead, "they live in the body" (17). I'll consider this concept further in the figure of the trans archive novel, and this is a distinct point of intersection between embodied minor archives and minoritarian mourning. In each instance, one mourns the past continually as the body persists. Later, Nadir wonders "how it would feel to inhabit my own body so fully that even the ache of fasting would feel miraculous" (37), as they come closer to that inhabitance, they become "a body without a past or a future, a pillar that bends light" (86). Nadir sheds one sense of body, but not of self, at a Black and brown queer dance party, at which they "bend and untangle and step out of my body," one of many "unruly bodies" in the room. The relative freedom of minoritized community celebration underscores a final axis of minor mourning of the body: control and release of embodiment and identity, with the freighted relationship between observer (member of various identitarian communities or not) and observed (comporting oneself toward said communities or not) that it carries with it. It is neither the correct haircut, nor the protection of Sabah (about whom Nadir wonder if she "finds it hard to stand being called a woman" (45) and understands Nadir's sex–gender before any of the other elders), nor even the careful love and support of friend-become-lover Sami that acts as tipping point for their realized embodiment. Instead, Nadir remains aware that "my body came with borders" (193), and thus their attachment to it rests between being inscribed within those borders and the uncertainty of losing them completely. *Thirty Names* has, on one hand, more complete resolution than many of these minor novels: Nadir's mother's ghost departs, the crew finds Laila and confirms the existence of the fugitive bird, Nadir and Sami's Arab community is more or less intact. But what remains staunchly unresolved is Nadir's "place in the world" in this minor sense of embodiment, identity, name.

The Trans Minor Mourning Novel

Minor literature can leave this copula open, frustrating the teleology and chronology of *Bildungsroman* and perhaps mourning narratives more broadly. Near the end of Megan Milks's *Margaret and the Mystery of the Missing Body*, its recently out trans protagonist writes about "The kind of girl who, at the same time as she is subscribing to cisheterofemininity at all costs, remains attached to the belief that she is special, is different, is exceptional; if anyone can master her body, she can. This is the ideal of white femininity, and it is sick" (254). Mastery is a telos, and as minor literature operates through deterritorialization, it leaves no space for masters. Instead, as these mourning novels demonstrate, the minor mourns the major for its shortcomings and frustrations, mourns the body for its responsibilities to majoritarian dictates, and mourns for its communities (and, by extension, self) when they are robbed of a life. In her trans revolutionary, TERF-defying *Manhunt*, Gretchen Felker-Martin offers a tender mourning scene between Fran and Beth, wherein the latter reflects, "Community is when you never let go of each other. Not even after you're gone" (256). Writing from and for minoritarian communities means leaving these points along axes of mourning unresolved and with sufficient traction to never be let go of. The architecture of a narrative arc that begins with birth, bends through development, and ends in death is both insufficient and out of step with lived experience. And so the minor reterritorializes mourning as embodiment through minoritarian community, the afterlife of subjectivity and subjecthood in those who live on. This reterritorialization is the difference between objectified memorialization and embodied memory, and each of these novels leaves the reader to wonder at the shapes and forms that the latter might take in the afterlife of each narrative. Trans minor mourning is Beth's refusing to let go of her community with Fran in a profound, formal sense: The ungrievable suffuses the narrative to such an excess that the minor subject does not, cannot, must not let go. The anti-normative potential is more than death not being the end; it is that trans minor becoming and community self-determination is a perpetual mourning and renewal.

4 The (Chosen) Family Novel

"Mother, brother, sister, family . . . seems like some kinda weird blood cult."
                                        (Jarboe, *Everyone on the Moon Is Essential Personnel*, 87)

"The family that we choose is sometimes more beloved than the family that is given to us."
                                        (McDonnell, *Poet, Prophet, Fox: The Tale of Sinnach the Seer*, 189)

From its earliest history in English, the novel and its genres have been dominated by family. The centrality of familial relationships and genealogy in eighteenth-century fiction – *Tristram Shandy, Clarissa, Tom Jones* – through to gothic classics – *Mysteries of Udolpho, The Monk, Vathek* – is unmistakable; the novel in English was a form birthed of the ability to deploy polyvocality and relationality through dialogue, exposition, and experiments with time. More canonical, thematic subgenres of long-form fiction such as the sentimental novel, courtship novel, or domestic novel often test structures and presumptions around family, but all are based on blood or the desire to formally/legally/religiously codify the expansion of family. The minor, by contrast, can turn these presumptions in on themselves, speculating on biological family or normativizing family roles in its characters' lives, as well as subsequent disidentification with and deterritorialization of said roles. In each case, the minor chosen family is offered less as a comparison to the normative, and instead occupies affective spaces unavailable to bio- or state-sanctioned family. The cultural rationality of family is transfigured into subcultures of communitarian care and extrafamilial relational structures. The genre resources of family novels are deterritorialized onto a spectrum of consent: How and why do minoritized subjects choose to distance themselves from biofamily and/or build resemblant formations according to trans minor subcultural rationalities?

The Shape of Biofamily in Trans Minor Literature

This section works from the geometries of biofamily in novels that focus on trans characters' positionality therein, and then turns to more radical departures from and refigurations of these shapes. But the ubiquity of biofamily in the form of the novel is worth addressing in some of the other novels in this Element first. This survey gives a sense of the general insufficiency of family to structure these novels or character development, even as a force to resist. These novels instead promote chosen family as smaller formations unto themselves.

In *Gray Heaven*, Jules is an orphan (born to "a woman who did not want me" [1]), and their state-sanctioned caretakers are foster families and group homes. Their deceased partner B, on the other hand, has a family that ranges from not unkind but ultimately disclaiming Jules's relationship with B to openly hostile and attempting to erase B's transness and queerness altogether. Jules has no family save for that assigned by the state; B has a family in death that they never really had in life. Jules experiences B's biofamily as a force that separates them from their great love, erases their relationship, and threatens legal action to prevent them from participating in mourning directly. Biofamily is an almost wholly abnegating force in this novel.

Little Blue Encyclopedia (for Vivian), includes Vivian's sister and her son with whom the narrator shares some of the grief around Vivian's death, as well as Vivian's parents who deadname and mispronoun their daughter in her obituary. Vivian's sister Dot and nephew Teddy are a source of some comfort for the narrator throughout the novel, but would be chosen family only by proxy; it is strictly the untimely death that has brought them together. Unlike Vivian's family, despite the fact that the narrator's parents and brother "weren't thrilled" about her being trans, "they eventually came around" (38). The parents are almost entirely offscreen for the novel, essentially irrelevant to the connection the narrator shares with Vivian, but brother Christopher appears at intervals, generally trying his best even as he fails to understand the narrator's mourning projects and transness. He apologetically misgenders her, and as she recounts her friendship with Vivian, recalls him "still coming to terms with me being trans" and not knowing "what to say or do around me" (89–90). Still, by the later time of the narrative, Chris and the narrator have a chummy relationship, going to a baseball game and birding together. He is a buffer of sorts between her and her parents and represents biofamily mostly staying out of the way.

Maria's family receives only oblique reference in *Nevada*, as she recognizes that even though her parents did not "beat gender normativity into me" (71), she had the impression from family that "My gender is wrong" (71). She later notes her sense of responsibility "for making sure her parents didn't have to have a weird kid" (98), but the parents never speak, there is no actual specific interaction to recall, and thus Maria's biofamily feels like an absented part of her history, perhaps something she outgrew, perhaps simply another structure of relationship to leave behind. Similarly, though James H. sees his mom "kind of a lot" (211), there is no sense of her presence in his half of the novel whatsoever. Family is defined mostly by absence.

Confessions of the Fox had its choice of pre-Victorian tropes of the loss of childhood/early-onset adulthood, and elected for young pre-Jack (identified only as P___) being sold into indentured servitude. Jack's mother's brief scene is enough to account for her as both bitterly poor and mostly cruel. Still Jack feels "unaccountable sympathy" as she leaves him, noting that "even if his mother looked at him with Horror, she looked at him" (15). He tries to recall her parting words and conjures a memory of the two of them walking along a riverbank, concluding ultimately "Better to just imagine Mum dead," as "Lots of urchins have lost their mothers" (17). So Jack is both chattel and orphan, unable to invent a different biofamily or to hear whispered stories of a saintly mother such as Oliver Twist's.

Biofamily must be contended with in each of these instances, but it does not structure the narratives, instead being most notable for its abnegation, its off-screen-ing, its absence, its inability to even be invented. Chosen family, on the other hand, manifests in various ways, but undergirds affective community through the degree and variety of choice involved. Some of the choices are presented as more likely due to proximity and shared experience, others are suggested to be more uncanny and happenstantial. But in each instance, a clear contrast is drawn between how biofamily could have structured these characters' narratives, against how chosen family (including the choice not to forge or maintain familial bonds) actually does. Family chosen along common lines of minoritization is insufficient to the brief of minor chosen family: Instead, the very forms of these novels centering on mourning, genealogy, self-actualization, and parentage are refracted and transformed through the significance of choosing one's closest kin. Trans minor chosen family novels ultimately speculate on what minor kinship can or must be for its characters to persist and thrive in their worlds.

The Vicissitudes of Biofamily in Mourning

Small Beauty's Mei is quite isolated, decamping from the city for the country-side and the cabin of her deceased aunt and cousin after the former's death. Using similar genre resources, we track a protagonist divorced from family and (nearly) alone in the city. However, in her city Mei does have a trans woman friend her own age in Annette and a generational trans elder in Connie. This chosen family is not exactly a unit, as the latter two women do not interact in any sustained way in the novel, but it does offer Mei a sense of home and belonging. The novel has shorn off Mei's biofamily by the time the narrative picks up, though we gain entree into these relationships through analepsis, memory, and haunting. Mei's father is absentee from young enough that she doubts she'd recognize him as an adult; her mother re-emigrates in close concurrence with Mei's coming out as trans; her maternal grandmother passes away somewhat unexpectedly; her aunt dies after battling terminal illness for some time; finally, her beloved cousin dies, totally unexpectedly after a work accident. This last loss is the most difficult of all, Mei noting "Sandy was the only relative she really had – blood relative, that is" (21). Mei thinks of family as "a tricky, shifting shoreline of a topic," as her "personal life has been pried into by community workers, doctors, counsellors, curious strangers, and police" (13). As a trans woman and second-generation migrant who has at least once been violently assaulted, is dealing with the loss of a string of biofamily and their residual earthly affairs, and requires routine doctor's visits for her gender-affirming care, Mei is entirely familiar with phobic state institutions and their entitlement to personal access. The result of this prying is an unwillingness or undesirability to discuss family with others who share her experiences: "She rarely brings up the topic with other trans women" (13). The two trans women she might bring it up with are very much chosen family; Annette is a constant source of good humor and encouragement, and Connie provides the wisdom of occupying subject positions of trans women and migrant for decades. This latter identity is critical for Mei, who marvels, "How amazing it is to meet someone like you who's older, when you've been living with the idea that no one like you ever gets to be older" (158).

Perhaps more than any other novel in this section, *Small Beauty* braids and muddles chosen and biofamily, creating an affective matrix of relationality through loss and what/who is left behind. Not long after decamping to the rather isolated house Sandy left Mei, she is encountered by Diane, who is revealed to be Sandy's mother Bernadette's former lover. In her grief, Mei is forced to contend with this overly gregarious and initially transphobic woman, as well as the revelation of her aunt's queerness. But for her part, "Diane does not know it but senses that Mei's arrival is an opportunity for penance" (116), penance for failing to see Bernadette as she died, penance for "guilt for not being there. Guilt for leaving" even before Bernadette was sick (111). In losing her – "without her broken relationship with Bernie, she doesn't have a thing" (111) – Diane is completely bereft of family and community. This does not stop her from bristling at Mei's transness, but even that prejudice ends up being insufficient to the desire to found a relationship with the relic of her lost love. When, Nelson, a queer friend of Diane's, is revealed to be potentially trans (139) upon his death, she apologizes to Mei, having found grounds to do so. These grounds include Diane's watching a documentary about a trans woman that "makes it more relatable" (121). Mei is incensed at the suggestion, telling Diane that these kinds of "stories" are an artifact of "some people [feeling] entitled to every-thing, the land we're on, who can stay, who has to go, what our lives are like" (121). Most devastatingly, Mei demands, "Why should I have to be relatable to get respect?" (121). Though Mei's initial formation is an intersectional, political one regarding migrancy and landownership, as well as queer and trans self-determination, the upshot is directly related to the concept of family. Relatability means legibility, and Diane and Bernadette's relationship, as well as the latter's impending pregnancy, gave way under the weight of Bernadette's mother's haranguing and Bernadette's fealty to her. Biofamily overwhelmed queer coupling, and a mixture of pride and hurt rendered Diane unable to offer comfort to her partner at the end of her partner's life. After all the loss she has experienced, it is almost unthinkable that Connie passes away while Mei is in her mourning, miles away. Mei is despondent, certain "she could have taken care of Connie like Connie had taken care of her" (129), mirroring Diane's doubled sense of loss – unable to see Bernadette out of guilt, then losing her permanently. And so the two women forge an uneasy sense of family, not exactly chosen, but bestowed through loss. The novel does not, however, deal in false equivalences regarding Diane's and Mei's subject positions. The former presents as butch, surrounded by men in work and sociality, and with the losses of Bernadette and Nelson, her entire queer milieu is evacuated. She hardly has family to choose from, and her unsuccessful attempts to relate to Sandy and marginally more successful attempts with Mei seem to be the extent of her efforts toward sympathetic community. But Mei has had an entire bloodline of women perish, and, even more devastating, has lost her closest consorts in Connie and Sandy. *Small Beauty* closes with a series of ghostly encounters as Mei takes Sandy's truck into the wilderness. These interactions allow Mei to enact not so much closure as perpetuated connectedness, begging the question of how biofamily especially changes in incorporeality. In the mourning section of this Element, we considered how minor community loss resonates in various ways through the stories that can be told after death. Here, Mei continues the stories directly with the deceased.

Sandy visits first, telling Mei he feels "like I haven't really left. Like most of me is still here" (140). Mei is unable to relate, perhaps because it is not clear where most of her is at this point. Just as with the other ghosts, there is an immediate familiarity and care from beyond. Grandmother Nai Nai is next, offering a kind of tutelage through a story about a beautiful forest that is ultimately interrupted when the idling truck backfires, and Mei drifts off again until Connie awakens her. At this, "Mei is confused. Ghosts of blood family somehow made sense, but Connie wasn't blood and besides, she had abandoned Connie. Maybe it was a punishment visit" (142). But Connie answers this thought directly: "People are connected through more than blood, you know this. And, for the record, you didn't abandon me" (142). As Mei continues to struggle with Connie's forgiveness, the older woman launches into her own story about a forest and how it regenerates from being burned. Connie has counseled Mei about her anger in many of their interactions on the earthly plane, now telling her it is the fire that will help protect her as well as see more things at which to be angry. Mei finds her way through her initial obstinance to ask the older woman if she dealt with her own fire (146). The rejoinder is somewhat grim, given the circumstances: "I'm dealing with it now" (146). Mei's ultimate regret remains related to abandonment and mortality, as she tells Connie "I'm so sorry I didn't know you better. Longer" (147). When Sandy's apparition returns, he expresses a similar regret around shared queerness, wishing that his mother and Mei "had got to know each other, you know, the way you really are" (157). Mei forgives Sandy because she has at least met Diane; Sandy forgives Diane "for being such a crap support to my mother" (157) in part because she is a "lonely, lonely woman" (158). Diane's complete lack of family, community, and affective relation makes her an object worthy of forgiveness, if not pity. Relatedly, it is herself that Sandy most desires Mei forgive. Sandy admonishes her to go back to the city, to Annette, her last remaining link to the independent life she was building. As Mei emerges from her revery, she feels herself "a moment on a spontaneous trajectory, her ancestors and descendants surrounding her, like water. Connected by blood and intention" (160). Still blood is not given the final word in *Small Beauty*; that is instead resolved for Annette's off-color joke about a pink canoe and plans to see Mei, who closes the phone conversation and the novel "Love you, too" (161).

Mei experiences the loss of biofamily as being cast of out time and gener-ation, though she has self-segregated from the phobic environments in which her family remains. The novel refuses to draw finer distinctions between the sources of violence (assault from strangers, incursions from the state, microaggressions from phobic publics), but they each think with chosen family – connections by more than blood – to consider forms of care and kinship (or the lack thereof) in identity and community non/formation. Self-determination and identity formation occur both despite and due to separation from biofamily, rendering death and disconnection formative markers of life and persistence, the minoritarian promise of forging kinships that help make sense of and sort through the lottery of biofamily, remapping familial care through fungible, renewable or revokable consent.

Surrogacy, Ephemerality, and Mutual Reliance of Chosen Family

Each of the protagonists of Casey Plett's *Little Fish* and Kai Cheng Thom's *Fierce Femmes and Notorious Liars* constructs, relies upon, and occasionally disidentifies with chosen family of trans femmes. Neither novel necessarily stages a binary relationship between biofamily and chosen family, but each forces the reader to contend with the complex relationship between biological lineage (which can be understood as vertical or clustered around a root) and chosen kinship (which is more horizontal and subject to the provisions of common interest, need, and other circumstances). This latter formation is certainly a covenant stronger than blood in both cases, though the ways in which the tendrils of chosen family curl back around memories and relationships of biofamily are important to both narratives as well. Thus, these examples are not so much contrastive as co-constitutive, neither seeking resolution nor relying on any singular, robust sense of family to define the protagonists or the microcommunities they construct, join, transgress, and change.

The topography of family is layered and knotty in *Little Fish*; the novel opens the night before the death of Wendy's grandmother; we meet Wendy at the bar with her trans femme chosen family, Lila, Raina, and Sophie. But within the first couple of chapters, Wendy has also received a call from an old friend of said grandmother who suggests that the longer-deceased grandfather was queer, and possibly trans as well. It is a very economically presented constellation of characters: protagonist Wendy, three members of closest chosen family, Wendy's chummy father Ben, two deceased grandparents, some extended family, and a distant relation bringing news of a genealogy of queerness heretofore unbeknownst to Wendy. Wendy has no memories of her mother, and relies on Ben to sporadically fill in details with stories. They drink together, they drink separately and run into one another at bars, they share thoughts and emotions and family history over beers; it is an unforced intimacy between them that can shift from dick jokes to deep empathy in the space of a brief exchange. With the femmes, Wendy shares experiences around trans health and sex–gender (medical elements such as hormones and surgery; sex work experiences; dating and sex), as well as a more social solidarity, going out together and aiding each other materially as needed or possible. Lila helps Wendy obtain medroxyprogesterone when she is unable to get a prescription through conventional channels and is Sophie's safe ride for a sex work appointment (as well as a safe call for Wendy's), lends Wendy her car to go see about grandfather's friend, and is the one to share the news of Sophie's suicide with Wendy. Raina is Wendy's roommate with whom she first shares the news about her grandfather; Raina is a consoling presence, always ready to offer coffee, beer, or company in the house they share with the two unnamed "cis roommates." She also offers Wendy counsel around her grandfather's potential transness, and Wendy in turn shares notes and care around Raina's impending bottom surgery. Near the end of the novel, Wendy and Raina are evicted and forced to find a new rental, ideally without the cis roommates. Wendy inquires, promising she'll "only ask this once, lady. What do you need from me now?" (284). It is a question that does not need to be asked more than once because it is a kind of permanent request, an open question in the sense that there need not be a final answer, if there even could be. Raina's answer is plaintive: "Keep me company through this miserable winter" (284).

As did *Small Beauty*, *Little Fish* confronts chosen family with loss and mourning. Wendy, Lila, and Raina are in the search party for Sophie when she goes missing and are later forced to mourn her together, "showered with condolences and queries and, strangely enough, friend requests" (167). Sophie's death is at the center of the narrative, and a great part of the novel is devoted not to understanding her suicide, but rather discovering what it means for someone to have left their chosen family, and how to persist with that absence. All fiction of familial loss, and perhaps suicide in particular, might involve an attempt at comprehension, but for chosen family it is multiplied: Why did one choose this relational unit? How, if at all, does their position in it change? Why do they choose to stay and why might they choose to leave? The Sophie we meet during the narrative is clever and raunchy and sad, and particularly acute around trans subjectivity and making her friends feel beautiful. Wendy's relationship with Sophie is especially emotive, and represents the shifting boundaries of the homosocial, the amative, the erotic, and the familial. As their hands touch in bed, Wendy momentarily feels "an overwhelming sense of peace, like the two of them were suddenly younger – much, much younger" (37). Chosen family implies the ability to choose the way one relates to family members in a manner not necessarily conscribed by social or cultural mores. The two women move back in time at one another's touch. Later, Sophie muses that she wish she'd known Wendy "back in the day" as she "didn't know any trans women growing up" (78). But in thinking back on her connection with Sophie, forged in a mere eight months, Wendy notes how they "had quickly become familiar with each other's roughnesses and edges, like siblings" (162). This siblinghood extends in different ways to Raina and Lila as well; Wendy again notes feeling "younger, much younger, like she had in certain fleeing moments when she'd hung out with Sophie" (271). This falling back into youth is elemental to chosen family: One can also choose the callowness or maturity with which one situates themselves in the familial relationship.

Sophie has depressive episodes throughout her time in the novel, but each of the women enacts or expresses affective issues at intervals; this is an important distinction that would read more strangely in a biofamily novel. Chosen family offers these subjects space to express mental and emotional health difficulties in the safety of one another's company, even if judgment of some kind may follow. Sophie is "taking it easy" as the femmes prepare to attend a costume party, but then "got blistering drunk the fastest" (28) and proceeds to hyperventilate and punch holes in a wall at dropping a dead flower she brought from home. This behavior is no more erratic or violent than what we witness from the other femmes, simply an opportunity to take care of Sophie the way they all take care of one another. This care is necessitated further by Sophie's increasingly dangerous sex work and, eventually, death. The femmes need to take care of Sophie's memory and others who knew her, just as much as one another. They are angry, frustrated, and hurt, in the sense that they cannot imagine having part of their family unit deducted. Sophie affirms her suicidality (45), and Wendy offers an experience with another trans friend who killed herself, though not as a prohibition, as "no one can stop anyone" (146). They move together forward in time as Wendy suggests "I want to grow old with you" (146).

But this is impossible, and the chosen family novel speculates on how radical consent and affirmation, rather than biological chance, might undergird familial closeness and responsibility. The novel as a form tends to operate along circuits of causality and progression, clear call-and-response within relationships (dis/loyalty, mutual or individual benefit, goodness and magnanimity or evilness and pathology); minoritarian responsibility and consequence can challenge linearity and majoritarian presumptions of progress, growth, and development. There is one particularly telling chosen-versus-biological family moment worth interrogating here that reflects this distinction. Wendy is struck by the still-recent passing of her Oma and in her own grief seems to forget that "Ben was probably still mourning" his mother as well (162). Families (chosen or otherwise) have mourning in common, though perhaps in more varied degrees and distances in biofamilies than chosen ones. The next chapter finds Wendy thinking of talking to her father, because though "he'd never met Sophie," Wendy "always thought she and Ben would see more of each other" (164). Wendy is fortunate to navigate between chosen and biofamily to the extent she sees fit. But this lost time with Sophie and Ben turns to thoughts of what she may miss from "her boy life" (165), namely "what she had had with her dad." When she meets Anna later, Wendy "wonder[s] if Sophie would've felt as much like a boy as she did just then" (247), a reflection on how relatively little of Sophie's prehistory Wendy has had the opportunity to learn. Herein lies one boundary line for Wendy's relationship with her father: He "had never been able to protect her as a girl," and, even worse, "Wendy had wanted that, always" (165). The chosen family is constituted to protect her as a girl, across a spectrum of ways, and now one of its members has left.

Wendy wonders what her father could "even relate to about my life now, anyway" (165). Another absence asserts itself in the cloud of familial relationality and loss: "Call your dad and tell him one of your best friends is dead. Call him. It's not like you have a mom. It's not like Raina or Lila or Sophie has dads!" (166). She quickly justifies this urge further. "Ben had good intentions; he loved her. He would want to hear from her. He would want her to reach out" (166). Despite the myriad ways in which biofamily cannot "relate" to Wendy's life, Ben and his daughter have experienced one of the biological realities of any family life – people will die. She has no mom to call; she should call him. Her chosen family members have no dads; she should call hers. Mourning Oma means reminiscing with the biofamily members who are still here and remembering the ways in which she touched their lives. Mourning Sophie is any uniform manner is almost an impossibility, as chosen family is forced to close ranks, discover how their fallen sister interacted with the world before she came into/helped form their family, and reconcile the ways in which she will remain with them for the balance of their own lives. Theirs is an empathic community, one of mutual support and aid, but its structure is not on set axes of care and control. Chosen family here disidentifies with fixed family roles, moving between sister (a kind of peer care through shared experience with authority and youth), mother–daughter (the former possessing experiential knowledge that the latter is assumed could draw upon in the future), and perhaps even an indistinct sense of father–daughter (only insofar as three of the four lacked fathers to speak of, and insofar as we read father as an alternative to mother). But this last point only further gestures toward undermining culturally transmitted family roles in chosen family. The trans minor challenge to family is not to replace it, but to expose its false superiority and deny its assumed biological significance and primacy.

While the presence and loss of elements of chosen family refract the protagonist's experience of biofamily and lineage in *Little Fish*, chosen family represents completely alternative paths away from biofamily and toward unknown horizons in *Fierce Femmes*. Choices regarding family are on a spectrum of pragmatism and provisionality for the unnamed narrator/memoirist of the novel. She seeks to write a story "about trans girls like you and me" (1), but proceeds to challenge this likeness through a mix of the danger and confabulation, coupled with affective reportage of experiences of leaving home, attaining sex-gender-affirming surgery, drug use, domestic dispute, and amative coupling. Each of these is shot through decisions around when to alter the terms of and/or leave family configurations. The arc of the narrative is open-ended and structured around a series of leavings: first, from childhood home and neighborhood. The narrator's biological parents fall in love in China, a "romantic story" that has turned to "broken dreams" and "an ever-present hunger" by the time the narrator is born (8). She notes, "When they looked at me and my sister, even their love was hungry" (8). As she expressed her wildness and femme-ness, the narrator's parents attempt to hold on "harder" (9), foretelling the second great escape of the novel (the first being from the boyhood foisted upon her). Throughout the bulk of the narrative, the narrator carries with her a swarm of killer bees, a pocketknife which serves to "open the mouths in my skin" when "there are too many insects" (19) beneath it, and a ghost friend, who is the only entity that can give her orgasms. The second escape, to the City of Smoke and Lights, is the nearly complete severing with parents (she does keep in touch with her mother via telephone), and her hometown of Gloom. The biofamily arrangement has failed her, though she feels protective over and corresponds with a younger sister back home. Her only other tie back to the family is her deployment of fighting skills and vigilant rage learned from her father, a former Shaolin monk and martial artist. Biofamily has given her innate anger and a way to physically enact it, as well as a smaller, blood-related femme over whom to watch.

Whether the narrator is actively seeking family upon her arrival in the City is debatable, but she does suggest that one can find "fierce, fabulous femmes … anywhere if you know how to look, and believe me, I am *looking*" (37). The progression of meeting, navigating, and ultimately escaping these femmes structures the bulk of the novel. There is the kind, matronly Kimaya, who observes in the narrator "a girl who is going to get herself in trouble" (37). Then we meet Kimaya's lover, the estimable Rapunzelle, followed by beautiful and biting Lucretia, Valaria the Goddess of War, and Alzena the Witch. The narrator depends on each of these femmes at intervals, and they often rely on her as well – the reciprocity of chosen family stems directly from participation by choice. The narrator's excitement that "anything can happen now that I am here with them" (39) is neither hyperbole nor a foregone conclusion: It is not the case that anything can happen with biofamilies in novels. The underlying blood link inflects each expression of relationship in a specific and bounded manner.

Kimaya is portrayed as "mother to a hundred girls" who "loved them, every single one" (153) in her station as organizer in the Femme Alliance Building. The narrator acknowledges Kimaya's inspiration and friendship, and confesses "I wouldn't have survived without Kimaya, her guidance and gifts" (152). Kimaya is not a second mother or surrogate; her familial orientation is a particular modality of care and actualization built around shared subject position and experience. At one of the more fraught interpersonal moments of the novel, Kimaya argues with ex-partner Rapunzelle about the results of the femmes' resistance campaign. The two of them alternate between parental and a more amative concern for the narrator, with Kimaya claiming "She deserves to have a normal childhood" (149), which Kimaya claims gang violence has taken away. Rapunzelle rejoins: "She lost the chance for the kind of normal life you're talking about before she was born" (149). The cliché of parentage implying making a better life for one's progeny runs up against the obstacles of phobic publics and their institutions; the "chance" for "normal" is forfeit even before birth. But what does chosen family offer in its place, if anything?

Rapunzelle is herself caring and gentle with the narrator, reenacting the model of Kimaya helping Rapunzelle through her addiction and loss of self. The narrator is touched and disbelieving, telling Rapunzelle "No one's this nice, not in real life" (44); whether it's real life, normal life, or another majoritarian/ normativizing heuristic, chosen family offers access to alternative territories for minoritarian survival and (relative) safety. Rapunzelle answers, "All the girls on the Street think they're so unique, but the truth is, we all come from the same story, more or less" (45). She offers the narrator a different sort of sisterliness, a shared history of abuse, and femme-actualization with someone who has perhaps more recently felt actualized. The narrator witnesses Rapunzelle and Kimaya's domestic strife around the tactics of the Lacerators gang, and despite (or possibly because of) Kimaya's "mission in life to make things better for us" (45), they separate acrimoniously. The roles shift between lover and co-organizer, sister and mother.

The familial community with fellow warriors Lucretia and Valaria is one of resistance to the phobic outside and affirmation through retribution. While Lucretia initially establishes superiority based on looks (51), she bonds with the narrator through killing a police officer who was preparing to murder Lucretia. Lucretia is the member of the family the narrator would least likely choose, but even there, the relationship is formative and adds contour to the familial experience. Valaria, on the other hand, is the de facto leader of the Lacerators and shares and fosters the narrator's taste for violence and combat.

Valaria is protective, but is eventually herself the one who has "to leave town for a while" (118) as the state violence closes in. She does so by kissing the narrator deeply, resulting in the narrator striking the larger femme in the face, leaving her bleeding but grinning at the provocation of erotically charged corporal punishment. The novel addresses the persistent issue of consent in chosen family throughout: consent to be taken care of, consent to allow a toxic person to stick around, consent to be drafted into a violent street gang, consent to be kissed.

The chosen family finally fractures around tactics, as if having a particular purpose (internalized care versus externalized revenge) overwhelms its bonds, breaking some, reinforcing others, leaving none unchanged. The unit shifts from one of protection and palliation to one of violence and shared power, and finally to a detente, which prompts the narrator's escape. After the initial schism, the narrator sees in Kimaya, "a part of her will never forgive this betrayal, not from Rapunzelle, not from me" (75). Families are not predicated on offering forgiveness, though chosen family may have higher stakes to do so. Kimaya's stakes are the highest, and the narrator goes on, "For a second, I am afraid that she won't survive it" (75). The initial enticement of gang misandry is strong, and after their first battle, the narrator is realized in a familial way. "Nothing has prepared us to feel this connected to one another, to feel this strong" (90). This is a sisterly strength, a transfeminist offensive against phobic publics. The strength is powerful, despite any reservations the narrator has regarding its foundation: "A part of me knows this can't possibly last – that sooner or later, they'll find out what I'm really like, and stop being my friends" (91–92). More than simple self-deprecation or manufactured uncertainty, the narrator notes the importance of choice in chosen family. Everyone gets to decide and negotiate the terms of care. As the wounds begin to heal within the community of femmes, the narrator notes: "I think we're relearning how to be friends, Kimaya and I: she's taking care of me less, and I'm trying to take care of her more" (158). This is not so much a lesson learned as it is the changing of terms of what chosen family can be for the narrator. And in the end, she exercises the consent to leave, as "not even a street full of beautiful sisters" is "strong enough to hold on to me forever" (186). Chosen family makes no overtures to being "forever," relying instead on the present and a sense of the ability to re/overwrite pasts as strategically or affectively necessary. In this case, the narrator draws the future into the past, a deterritorialization of time and the concept of family in fiction: "I am leaving them so I can love them. I am going so that I can return" (186). The genre resources of family as the ties that bind are reterritorialized onto chosen family as the ties that can be severed and restitched selectively.

Re/productive Choice, De/transition, Re/familialization

Torrey Peters' *Detransition, Baby* tracks the rise, climax, and denouement of a three-parent chosen family arrangement, thematizing consent, renarrativization, and fetishization of queered parentage and partnership. The novel offers evidence, however, that it was always about the parentage and never really about the partnership, a unique way to speculate queer chosen family. The three members of this unit operate from various conceptions of both choice and family, changing position relative to one another as the novel progresses. Initially and most persistently throughout the narrative, it is Ames who seeks a designed arrangement with ex-girlfriend Reese to raise the potential child with which he has impregnated Katrina. Reese is most skeptical of the entire concept of this family arrangement, but is deeply desirous to become a mother, paying down a complex of emotions around the inability to become pregnant, the stigma around trans women as (especially single) parents, and the unlikelihood of otherwise participating in biological parentage. For her part, Katrina's pregnancy is a surprise, rendering her winnable to the concept of an additional co-parent. As the novel progresses, she is further won through the concept of participating in queerness and the ways in which this arrangement helps vindicate her divorce from a cis man. But Ames, now years on from his breakup with Reese and having detransitioned (without initially making Katrina aware of that part of his history), longs for family both as an abstraction and as a manner of bringing Reese, who mothered Amy through her earlier transition and prides herself on having mothered other younger trans women. Of course, she was not only mother, as "her first trans daughter – Ames – had also been her lesbian lover. Amy. A daughter whom Reese had raised to love Reese well as a wife, with all the strange dynamics in power that entails, the dynamics that are so confusingly sexy and painful and satisfying and awkward that the rest of society has an incest taboo to avoid them" (88). It is only incest if the family is "real" or "actual," and Reese's accounting for the nature of their relationship makes it so.

Nevertheless, in this chosen family reading I want to focus on some of Ames's reflections on choice and perhaps why the family unit never comes to full fruition, as the novel leaves us with Katrina speculating on terminating the pregnancy. Incestuous or not, Amy and Reese's relationship was formative both romantically and in terms of her sense of woman-ness (if those two are separable to begin with). Peters also baits the reader into considering a causal relationship between the end of their coupling and Ames's detransition, a choice that in a certain sense leads to the pregnancy to begin with. Early on, the novel justifies why someone would choose to co-parent with an ex who will not be biofamily to the child. "When Ames thinks hard about Reese," he feels a spectrum of emotions, including shame, due to an inability to explain "what he still wants from her" (16). He concludes that, in contradistinction to romantic feelings, "he misses her in a familial way," and more specifically, "in the way he missed and felt betrayed by his birth family when they cut off contact in the early years of his transition" (16). Ames has decoupled chosen/longed-for family from romantic feelings, and instead mirrored losing his birth family to transition with losing his chosen family to detransition. The provocation of the limits of queer and trans chosen family is perhaps most legible in contradistinction to some of the chosen family structures detailed in the novel. Ames thinks of his abandonment as "more adolescent than that of jilted adult romantic love," though he certainly was jilted at their parting. Still, the loss of the familial link supersedes the romantic. Ames shares Reese's sense of their coupling. "Reese hadn't just been his lover, she'd been something like his mother," and the kind of mother she was involved teaching "him to be woman . . . or he'd learned to be a woman with her" (16). Peters leaves open whether this chosen family originates more through Reese's maternal or erotic capacities, but then again, the incestuousness leaves room for both simultaneously. When one adds in the reiterated timeline of hormones and transition, the blurring becomes even more pronounced: Reese "had found him in a plastic state of early development, a second puberty, and she'd molded him to her tastes. And now she was gone, but the imprint of her hands remained, so that he could never forget her" (16). The reader is offered almost nothing of Ames's biofamily, only that it was "a chain he'd voluntarily decoupled from in order to breathe" (108) – and so the only lasting imprints and molding are those of Reese. He cedes a great deal of control to her here, and even more so in his desire to bring her back into his orbit.

Ames returns to this line of thinking as he justifies co-parenting with Reese, "the trans woman from whom he'd learned about womanhood" (37). The choice of verbs here is notable: He "learned about" womanhood, rather than "learned to be" a woman, despite the fact that this was clearly tutelage with praxis. The complexity of this familial relationship deepens as Ames speculates on the triangle he is proposing. On one hand, "It had only ever been through her, with her, that he could imagine parenthood" (37); it is both "through" and "with" her that qualifies his consideration of parenthood. On the other hand, Ames is certain Reese "would see his fatherhood and dismiss it" as, "To her, he would always be a woman" (37). Her (first) motherhood fails if she acknowledges Ames's man/fatherhood, something she essentially refuses to do throughout the novel. But the surrogacy is not simply of parenthood: "By borrowing her vantage, he could almost see himself as a parent," and Reese's presence would cancel out his being a father, which is somehow unacceptable to him as well. Ames is totally clear on the choice at this stage, as "what he wanted anyway" is "to be family with Reese once more, in some way" (37). A transfeminist reading here may be muddy (Is this behavior manipulative? Codependent? Radical in deterritorializing cisnormative parentage?), but the minoritarian chosen family reading is clear – Ames will elect to overwrite the loss of his biofamily with the reimplementation of his chosen one, a family that never had the role of father available or necessary. Still, Ames recognizes the strangeness, the queerness of the valve this parentage represents for him. Whereas Reese and Katrina "get what they wanted" in the form of a baby and a commitment from a lover, respectively, Ames's reward is "to live up to what they both hoped he could be by being what he already was: a woman but not, a father but not" (37). Chosen family is the conduit through which Ames's liminality or non-definition can persist.

Furthermore, the destabilization of the heteronormative, nuclear family is particularly paramount for both Katrina and Ames. Ames pitches the arrangement to Reese as "confusing enough to break the family thing," but with her influence "could be a family that works" (37). But the question of "works" is left open to the point of total unclarity: There is no appropriate model to reference, there are only different prospects and degrees of failure. This minor literature is especially adept at non-resolution, or what we might term irresolution, always forestalling the possibility of family working to the point of parody. Ames seeks this arrangement from a place of hurt, and it is left unclear the extent to which he thinks co-parenting with the two women will somehow concretize his own identity and embodiment. He implores Reese, "If we weren't meant to be lovers, it doesn't mean that we weren't meant to be family" (44). Ames's gender failure is shared with Reese, and now his familial failure (that is, failure to be a father) will be as well. In this turbulent moment, he reveals the grandest deterritorialization of chosen family: "If we don't try again, it's like our time together . . . Not only did it end, it was like it never was" (44). Chosen family has the ability to overwrite and extend the past, reterritorializing the erotic onto the familial. Near the end of the novel, Reese's friend Thalia announces "that she had spent the night thinking about Reese's problem" – that Katrina may excise Reese from the arrangement, or not have the baby at all – "and that it was not in fact a problem, but a solution. Ames and Katrina had indeed been the issue all along. Reese was a queer, if she was going to do a queer family model, she ought to do it with real queers" (309). To the outside observer, Ames and Katrina are insufficiently queer, not least because their family is insufficiently chosen. Biological accident and Ames's failure to inform Katrina of the likelihood of pregnancy has bonded them, and Thalia reads Reese as incidental or at best supplemental to the biofamily relation. But regardless of whether the geometry of this family is queer enough or even chosen enough, it short-circuits the novel's sense of defined roles and the verticality of lineage versus the horizontality of sibling-hood and coupling. In so doing, it also deterritorializes mourning from loss to grieving what has not yet been or cannot ever be – Reese mourns the mother-hood that seems forever out of reach and politically, culturally, and personally barred.

But *Detransition, Baby*'s frustrated chosen family also puts pressure on the archive of the body: Katrina is under the yoke of her lost marriage and the status of divorcée, Ames of his lost transition and his repositioning as masc, and Reese of the fetishization of her trans feminine body and the child it cannot bear her. The novel refuses them the "magic bullet" arrangement that might fulfill each of these aspirations and leaves the reader to decide what it means if we were expecting them to work out in the first place.

The Trans Minor (Chosen) Family Novel

There are generational veins of queer, feminist, and trans criticism that enumerate and expose the violence of biofamily, and perhaps an equally voluminous body of work on the triumphs and travails of queer chosen family. To think of biofamily as a structuring generic principle for a novel is straight-forward enough, as is to think its absence or denial. But the strange and minor uses to which this trans minor literature deploys the generic resources of the family are almost never as simple as rejection or contrast. *Small Beauty* annihilates its protagonist's biofamily, bifurcating Mei's experience of chosen family who know her only as a trans woman and biofamily who experienced her transition and reacted in a spectrum of ways. The novel deterritorializes the primacy of filial attachment and devotion and revokes Jun's mother–child relationship with Mei, as the latter understands her transition as causally linked to the former's exiting her life forever. Not wholly dissimilarly, *Fierce Femmes* uses the thematic of escape to narrativize the insufficiency of family: The narrator escapes her biofamily, then her femme chosen family, then her amatively coupled chosen family. These familial arrangements are important for the terms of their leases, as the narrator learns to fight, then leaves; to love, then leaves; to orgasm, then leaves. None of the relationships is romanticized as undergirding the narrative as a whole. Both Reese of *Detransition, Baby* and Wendy of *Little Fish* have their trans femme chosen families, and each novel experiments with interruptions to these unit – factors outside the initial choices to forge familial bonds. In Reese's case, chosen family with Amy is blown apart by a broken relationship and the latter's detransition; the next iteration by Katrina's phobias and Ames's inability to intervene in either of their better interests. Whatever drama Reese makes for herself is amplified by the prospective family members with which she surrounds herself. Wendy's biofamily and chosen family each lose a key matriarch unexpectedly to death, and thus Wendy is forced to modulate between looking to the remaining members of each for consolation. It's a structure of feeling that muddles the ties that bind, as Sophie's decision to leave chosen family is impossible for Wendy to fully comprehend. The trans minor (chosen) family novel can at once challenge the supremacy of biofamily, speculate on and celebrate its replacement, and mourn the insufficiencies of both.

5 The Archival Novel

> "Down, down, down in the archives, down in the archives we bury all the answers, all the dirt, all the tar, all the answers. Down, down, next to the bunker, through the deep tunnel, close to the uranium, that's where you go, that's where you go when you must know."
>
> (Lake, *Future Feeling*, 211)

> "I have to say, as archivists, we let people down when we pretend to be objective. We help them when we admit what we don't know. And those can look like the same thing, but they're opposite things."
>
> (Fellman, *Dead Collections*, 160)

Finding Trans History

What does a minor historical novel look like in the popular absence of a minor history? Leslie Feinberg, in *Transgender Warriors*, sought to rectify the nonexistence of a trans historiography as both a committed Marxist who sought a materialist history to trace the sociopolitical conditions of hir present, and as a non-cis person who sought to excavate other "transgender warriors" to bolster hir own sense of identity and endurance in the record. Before engaging in the project of transgender history in earnest: "I couldn't find myself in history. No one like me seemed to have ever existed" (11). The historical novel could be seen as a modality of repair for the inability to find oneself; where the record is vacant, simply invent. But this was not Feinberg's path (despite the ways in which each of hir novels acts as historical intervention). Instead, "It is time for us to write as experts on our own histories," zie wrote, as "For too long our light has been refracted through other people's prisms" (xii). Of course, these aims could apply as a method for aesthetic production just as well as political praxis or social science research. But Feinberg, as an accomplished author of explicitly political tracts as well as long-form fiction and participant ethnographic research, chose to write a history in addition to hir other work. The impetus:

"to fashion history, politics, and theory into a steely weapon with which to defend a very oppressed segment of the population" (xii). Can a historical novel attempt these same ends?

Twelve years after the publication of *Transgender Warriors*, Susan Stryker published another landmark in codifying transgender history in the United States. Her book *Transgender History* focused "specifically on the history of trans and gender nonconforming social change activism in the United States – that is, on efforts to make it easier and safer and more acceptable for the people who need to cross gender boundaries to be able to do so" (12). While Feinberg sought trans identities in the broader historical record, Stryker looked to create a finding aid for the archive of trans activism and social justice. Less a playbook for trans activism than a communitarian memory of struggle, Stryker's history moves past simply locating non-cis subjects and on to thinking with their forms of struggle and resistance. In both cases, though, the authors indirectly cast doubt on the project of a minor historical novel, or at least one with the kind of political charge that this exercise in thinking genre seeks. Feinberg (*Transgender Warriors*) notes, "Today, a great deal of 'gender theory' is abstracted from human experience" (xiii), something zie had little time for as an organizer and, frankly, theorist. Zie continues, "But if theory is not the crystallized resin of experience, it ceases to be a guide to action" (xiii). As such, a Marxist materialist history of minoritarian subjects must reflect that experience directly and forcefully. And so Feinberg, similar to Stryker, offers "history, politics, and theory that live and breathe because they are rooted in the experience of real people who fought flesh-and-blood battles for freedom," a worthy exercise in and of itself, but the final modus is the one that separates my understanding of a historical novel from something else. Feinberg concludes, "And my work is not solely devoted to chronicling the past, but is a component of my organizing to help shape the future" (xiii). Not simply chronicling the past, nor inventing it, but seeing it as elemental to imagining and working toward better futures. Stryker (*Transgender History*) offers a not dissimilar note regarding durative distance and history. "The closer the past approaches to the present, the easier it is for the welter of fleeting events to obscure the larger contours of the times we are living through" (170). Of course, which events are fleeting and which are instructive regarding these contours remains up for debate; phobic, majoritarian epistemology is premised on selection criteria regarding history and possible futures. The historical novel cuts a path through legible pasts to orient the reader to their moments. Trans minor understandings of history are less beholden to this legibility as they question the presumed good of visibility, representation, and codifiable/categorizable status.

The Incommensurability of a Minor Historical Novel

Another Marxist cultural historian and theorist, Georg Lukács, wrote a dense and definitional history and theory, *The Historical Novel*. Part of the work of this study was to detail ways in which the form had changed and perhaps ceased to be possible in the manner Walter Scott deployed it a century and a half earlier. In thinking of the future prospects for the historical novel, Lukács writes: "We see that all problems of form and content alike in the historical novel of our day" – that day being in 1937 –

> centre upon questions of heritage. All aesthetic problems and valuations in this sphere are determined by the struggle to liquidate the political, ideological and artistic heritage of the period of declining capitalism, by the struggle to renew and fruitfully extend the traditions of the great progressive periods of mankind, the spirit of revolutionary democracy, the artistic grandeur and popular strength of the classical historical novel. (332)

Lukács's historical novel is indeed a grand and popular form, which already qualifies minor uses. But the struggle to revise, destabilize, and problematize the heritages he lists are part and parcel of the minor and trans minor genre uses in particular. One of the enduring characteristics of Lukács's literary analysis is the tightrope it walks between the formal and critical-philosophical. It is thus notable when he suggests the historical novel's apparently "purely formal, compositional problems – e.g., whether the great figures of history should be principal heroes or minor figures – so obviously conceal ideological and political problems of the highest importance" (332). The problem of "whose history?" and the appropriate emphases end up being a veil or even a diversionary tactic, another way to elide the minoritarian and the minoritized. Lukács then offers a further case against the station of the minor within this genre designation: "Indeed, the whole question of whether the historical novel is a genre in its own right, with its own artistic laws or whether it obeys essentially the same laws as the novel in general can only be solved on the basis of a general approach to the decisive ideological and political problems" (332). This version of the historical novel of "today" is just The Novel, meaning the majoritarian novel, the "great (and established)" traditions and lineages that are self-reinforcing and recursive.

But Lukács's final declamation of a modern historical novel offers the opening for the alternative I propose. He suggests that "The historical novel of the humanists of our day is closely linked with the great and urgent problems of the present. It is on the way to portraying the *prehistory of the present*" (337), which could be an answer to Feinberg's call to operationalize theory, but could just as easily be the artifact of the progressivist history of the majority. Lukács is skeptical of these efforts: "The humanist historical novel of today gives only an abstract prehistory of ideas and not the concrete prehistory of the destiny of the people themselves, which is what the historical novel in its classical period portrayed" (337). I suggest we consider a trans minor counter to the historical novel in the figuration of an archive novel, whose indices and instruments are designed for and operated by minoritarian subjects to wield their own senses of pastness and where to break from it, rearrange it, squirrel it away into, or excavate it from the archive for examination. The archive novel, as I conceive it, is initially structured around similar benchmarks to the historical novel: accuracy (including "correcting" the record), authenticity (following the historical "rules"), and fictionality/texture (why bother writing fiction if the history is available?). To these, though, the archive novel distinctly adds revelation (the responsibility to present something new without sacrificing accuracy/authenticity), and also a correspondent fathoming of depth (how much is actually out/in there?).

In the scope of this Element, it is more worth speculating on minor genres and forms of archives rather than the simple existence of actual, physical or digital archives – there is a strong and growing number of archives and collections in North America whose mission is to collect women's, queer, and/or trans histories (although without question the last of these is the fewest). But a minor archive is built almost in converse to an encyclopedic historical archive based on place, era, or subject. Its collections are often the discarded, devalued, or overlooked ... the excess or the subaltern even around or within existing archives. If a minor historical novel would be by nature insertive, structured around a "contemporary" perspective on older events/ideas/people, then the minor archive novel is fabulated, exctractive/excavative and deterritorializing, structured around both the uncanniness of archival research and correspondences with unknown pasts.

A Note on Derrida's Feverish Fictions

The (somewhat?) hyperbolized fictional publishing conglomerate "P-Quad" deploys one of its corporate henchmen to accost the narrator/annotator Professor Voth of *Confessions of the Fox* upon his university's discovery that he has happened on to and been given (in the course of the university's liquidation of its library) a rare eighteenth-century account of the trans masc thief, Jack Sheppard. Said corporate henchman, Sullivan, represents the newly expanding pharmaceutical company's "Archival Text Authentication Division" (84), which he claims is modeled on "Derrida's view that 'Archival meaning is also and in advance codetermined by the structure that archives'" (84). Voth is at once aghast at this "violence" against Derrida (84), and at the same time cannot argue with the brutal capitalist/colonialist logic of P-Quad's design, in short: "With your footnotes you'll . . . add labor to the document. Invent, if you will" (122n), which will allow P-Quad to take ownership of the manuscript. I do not need to rehearse Derrida's study in full here, but I would like to consider the extent to which the titular *Mal* of his *Mal d' Archive* is a fictional one. Analyzing Yerushalmi's letter to the long-dead Sigmund Freud, Derrida (*Archive Fever*) speculates on the fictionality of interacting with an archival figure that apparently cannot answer back: "This fiction has another originality, which sets the fictionality . . . as if *en abyme*" (39). In its being addressed to a deceased person, "the historian's object became spectral subject" (39), which Derrida accounts as "another archival effect" (40). The minor subject is spectralized in various ways, through elision, overwriting, and illegibility. A minor archive, then, might be a fiction constructed in the discourse between a spectral subject and a spectral historian. Derrida continues, regarding this effect, that "In its very fiction" the letter "enriches the corpus it claims to treat but which it enlarges and of which, in fact, it is henceforth a part" (40). Whereas Voth's interaction with the manuscript is to render it sufficiently "original" for the majoritarian/corporate/academic world, for the minoritarian communities to which he addresses his footnotes it becomes a matter of enlargement and integration with the past. Derrida later suggests of the archive that "It is not the contents of this 'historical novel'; it is rather the scene of reading it provokes and in which the reader is inscribed in advance" (67). In the case of the archival novel, the writer-historian is the reader, inscribing subjects out of the documents and objects of an under-curated vault of pastness. Susan van Zyl ("Psychoanalysis and the Archive") notes that Derrida's accounting of the latter "has to do with the question of the future" (40) as well, "the archive as being not simply a recording of the past, but also something which is shaped by a certain power, a selective power, and shaped by the future, by the future anterior" (40). Part of how the archival novel shapes the future is just by thematizing and manipulating selective power. Van Zyl stresses, "the fiction is an important point" in the letter to a dead man, a point echoed by Ronald Suresh Roberts ("Keeping the Self"), who notes that, in the archive effect, "fiction secretes, it extrudes, fact that is not merely found but also at once made" (305). Archival fictions extrude, minor archival novels cut from whole cloth facts of experience, the fruits of trans minor epistemologies and measures of truth. Roberts concludes, of these archival fictions, "Beginning in imagination, in the intangible, fiction ends in positivity" (305), assumedly in the sense of creating something that was not there. But an archive novel suggests that there is a mass already there, from which fiction secretes and fact is extruded.

We have perhaps moved from archive fever to a duller (but no less impactful) archive anxiety, as nervous and frustrated by what we are sifting through as by what we might or might not find. Fabulating and speculating on the gaps in actual historiography serves one set of purposes (cf. Saidiya Hartman's answer to archival silencing), but fictionalizing and deterritorializing history itself serves another. The minoritized historical novel becomes the minor archive novel at the moment it refuses to conceal its ahistoricality and irreality. The lost trans subjects are not found and recuperated, or even inserted into history; history is instead reformulated around the minor subjects themselves. The genre materials of reported histories and historical likelihood are deterritorialized onto archival memory and revaluation of fact and fiction to understand and account for pastness.

Archives as Confessions of Desire

Confessions of the Fox is comprised as much of Voth's confessions of self-doubt, relationship destruction, and frustrations with his station in the academy as those of the titular "fox," Jack Sheppard. In the midst of these frustrations, the archivist notes being "Caught up in the manuscript" (259n), the result of which is forgetting "a central tenet of decolonial theories of the archive – its critique of our fetish for archival truths" (259n). Minor novels confront fetishes in various ways, as we have seen, using genre as a tool to expose and reformulate both constructive and destructive fetishes around trans subjects. Voth goes on to cite Anjali Arondekar's description of the archival fetish that "if a body is found, then a subject can be recovered" (259n), but in the case of the Sheppard manuscript, "There is no (one) body in this archive, no one subject either." The novel is at once an archival interrogation of this often-revelatory manuscript and Voth's own archive of (and archival) feelings, his senses of masculinity and sex, his powerlessness within institutions and his empowerment in the abolition thereof. The central hinge is between how little has actually been known of Sheppard in the past (and it is worth noting here that the "autobiography" of the actual John Sheppard sold at his execution in 1724 is presumed to be written by the great and established novelist Daniel Defoe) and how much of this manuscript has been annotated and altered through the years of its existence. Voth notes, regarding the scarcity of information about Jack's lover, Bess, that "Researchers have long been forced to source her 'truths' in the Sheppard works, in which she appears regularly, albeit in a variety of shifting forms. (Though, caveat: this profound lacuna in the records cannot be simply filled; it must be encountered head-on as constitutive of the archive as such.)" (31n). The difference between filling a lacuna and encountering it head-on as a constitutive feature is a dichotomy unique to minoritarian archives for which extant narratives do not exist to be deployed into the gaps. The archive fiction is not filling these gaps but tracing their borders and challenging their negative spaces. In the case of *Fox*, so much of the archive of eighteenth-century queer and trans masc experience is either incomplete or posthumously encountered through generations of radical archivists. Jack's deadname (and sex-gender assignment at birth), a missing textbook photo of the genitals of a "chimera," the various alterations and emendations of the Stretchers, the embedding of a radical translingual slogan ("Pa ni mèt ankô"), and even the closing line of the manuscript – Voth's one confessed addition – "And go with her" (315) are each examples of such encounters, the archival effects of uncovering minoritarian histories that require fabulating and expanding into the available vessel – in this case, the novel.

But this archival encounter is mediated through a specific communitarian intervention, that of the Stretchers, offering access to "a marvelous set of materials" (266n) and having "collected so much on us" that they are "not exactly archivists" (267n) but something more authorial. As Voth himself stretches to access the descriptive language necessary to detail the Stretchers' work, he offers insight into how history can be extended through the minor archive to encounter minoritized subjects. Rebekah Edwards considers "questions about the potential extension of the narratives of normativity" attached to the production of items that could be appropriated for a trans archive (652). But Rosenberg encounters this concern by deploying the fictionality of a trans archive through normative (i.e., colonial, carceral) narratives of history; he authors a novel that produces a trans character out of history. Edwards goes on to wonder "What problems might arise when we seek to wrest trans* artifacts from archives that organized or produced those artifacts as part of a strategy to classify certain bodies as deviant, problematic, or Other in order to consolidate ideas about 'normal' embodiment?"(652–653), to which Professor Voth might reorient the verb "wrest," which implies excavation and extraction against phobic forces, to "stretch," in his accounting of the mantra of the Stretchers: "All history should be the history of how we exceeded our own limits" (267n). The minor archive novel sets both the limits and the mechanics of exceeding them. Of course, Voth invokes not just minor or minority history, but "all history," which suggests the impossible complete archive of the past that has limited and limned minoritized subjects; a trans minor archive includes both a history of trans subjecthood and the artifacts of both being and having been. Voth was "told there were once lively debates here about whether or not it was even worth collecting any of our histories at all" because "After all, what are we but the accumulation of centuries of terror?" (267n). The historical novel might document this terror, to learn from the past in hopes of not repeating it or other such clichés that neoliberalism offers the subject positions it has subalternized. The decisive distinction, which gives rise to the minor archival novel, is a temporal one, as Voth avers, "In our terrible past, my new friends see a different future reflected like light off broken shards" (267n). The minor archival novel presents a minor reading practice that simply refuses the linear, progressivist narrative of history; it finds the future in the past and vice versa, a dialectic of becoming(s). Thus, when Voth goes on to explain why the Stretchers refer to their material and curation thereof as "stretches" rather than archives, he notes "they mean stretches of time, but also stretches of space. And they don't just mean space as a place; they mean space as a practice: the way we make space in our own bodies" (267n). Time stretches between past and future, space between place and practice; the minoritarian subjects make space in their own bodies, but space for what? To the Stretchers, Voth concludes, "this is history: breathing air into a previously unfelt opening" (267n).

Confessions of the Fox does, in fact, track a kind of progression through its archival discovery and invention, but it is not the one the reader of a historical novel might expect. The revelation of Jack's transness is almost immediate, and even his great, epiphanic love affair with Bess is instantiated quickly. No, it is Voth's political awakening and sense of his own capacity for resistance that develops through his running commentary in the footnotes. By the time he joins the Stretchers, he is indeed something in excess of archivist, he adds his own stretches and guesses at those added before. Voth has in essence enacted a version of Arondekar's stock-taking, that "For better or for worse, the archive has emerged as the register of epistemic arrangements, recording in its prolifer-ating avatars the shifting tenor of debates around the production and ethics of knowledge" (2). The ethics of this archive novel begin with curiosity (as they must), proceed through discovery and identification (of and with Jack, details around the carceral city and the sexual and racial diversity of underground London), encounter capitalism and the commodification of knowledge, and end with abolition of police, academia, capitalism, and, finally, progressivist, inev-itable history itself. The tenor of this debate moves from one of ownership of history to what that history actually is/means/does.

Archives as Invitation into Disbarred Pasts

In detailing the charge of the Digital Transgender Archive that K. J. Rawson helped cofound, the site suggests using "the term transgender to refer to a broad and inclusive range of non-normative gender practices. We treat transgender as a practice rather than an identity category in order to bring together a *trans*-historical and *trans*-cultural collection of materials related to *trans*-ing gender" (Digital Transgender Archive). Just as minority is imparted onto communities or subject positions, minoritarian is a set of practices deterritorializing and taking flight from the majoritarian. Rawson ("Archive") notes elsewhere that "The intersections of transgender phenomena and the archive … involve both a material dimension (the collecting, maintaining, and accessing of transgender historical materials in a physical repository) and a theoretical dimension (the power dynamics, political motives, epistemological function, and affective currents of any archival project)" (24). It is these theoretical dimensions that fiction can uniquely engage, deploying its affinity for affect and epistemological experimentation to display archival effects. In harmony with the epigraph from *Dead Collections*, Rawson goes on to note how "Far from a neutral or objective record of the past, a transgender archive is thus a rhetorical institution that is intentionally adapted to an audience for a particular persuasive purpose" (25). A novel is a rhetorical institution as well, an entry into a relatively lengthy and voluminous history, even as certain subjects and subjects positions remain ghostly, spectral, or underdeveloped therein. Shola von Reinhold's *LOTE* makes no pretense of neutrality, as its minor subjects are interested in constructing archives that offer them some sense of identification in history, in this case a particularly nefarious, concealed history. Rawson sees this concealment as endemic: "The selection and discrimination involved in archiving creates a residual silencing of others" (25). And there are of course different strategies for encountering the "centuries of terror" that Rosenberg notes. Rawson asks, "And what of the history that is hoped to be forgotten? Transgender people who transition their gender presentation may feel betrayed by the archive's stubborn and insistent refusal to forget" (25). In *LOTE*, the latent, waiting revelation is around the difference between forgetting and willful amnesia, archival smothering and minoritizing subjects into the marginalia of the dustbin of majoritarian history.

Finding/Becoming the Archival Other

Archive explorer Mathilda volunteers alongside Elizabeth/Joan (the double-naming due to the former being past the point of propriety in asking which is actually the latter's name) in an unnamed archive under an apparently disused gentleman's club in London. The two of them interact with relatively few people in the small archive, among them Agnes, a woman in her eighties who "enjoys it as much I did" (40) and the only other Black person working in the archives. When Elizabeth/Joan discovers Mathilda is not actually researching a sanctioned biography, the employee accuses the volunteer of being, like Agnes, "one of the Necrophiles!" (45). To someone drawing a nominal wage from the institution, the only way Elizabeth/Joan can understand unwaged interest in old things is fetishistic and weird. But Mathilda's necrophilia is not a generalized interest in or desire for the past; it is directed at recognizing herself as out of time and place in various registers, a Black, potentially trans "at certain points I thought of her more consciously as a trans-femme character, and at other times much less consciously" (Von Reinhold, "Interview") woman aesthete for whom beauty and decadence are life forces that she sees reflected back in a certain social circle or society living the afterlife of fin de siècle aestheticism. Mathilda's interest in the figure of Stephan Tennant and other "Bright Young Things" is expressed in the form of "Transfixions," a kind of ecstatic identification by contrast with the decidedly not bright present. These transfixions are the initial central epistemological form of the novel, Mathilda taking notes on the "sensations" experienced from each photo she collects. As Mathilda combs through a box of photos, she recognizes Bloomsbury Group personalities, including Virginia Woolf, and, finally an unrecognizable Black woman with Tennant, Hermia Druitt (29). Hermia is "a new Transfixion" with whom Mathilda feels "an almost violent familiarity" (31). Mathilda's archive of Transfixions achieves a new dynamic with the discovery of Hermia, after which Mathilda pursues a mysterious residency program that turns the compulsion to research these figures into making her "look like an artist" (64). And in fact, Mathilda's archival practice may be an act of invention, as she wonders: "Did it matter if they had been real people?" (48). But it does matter, or at least it matters if they could have been. Just as Jacques's *Variations* animates trans para-histories from both plausible and aspirational elements of the past, so too does Mathilda invent herself into the past with which she is Transfixed. I argue that this developing ability/strategy to imaginatively identify with the past is particular to the minor, uniquely accessible at the margins, which are perhaps more fixed (in terms of phobias against minoritized subjects) across preceding generations than is the majoritarian center.

As Mathilda carves out her space in the Residency, she finds Erskine-Lilly, a character who has taken Mathilda's fixations to a Wildean limit of living aesthetically. They are "A living transfixion" (261), who has secreted themselves away in a shell of decadence near the Residency. Their space is an archive of another lifestyle, one more in contact with and in search of other transfixions, cases of champagne and "a load of brocade furniture" Mathilda "did not have a name for" (255). Put another way, "Everything that was not part of Erskine-Lilly's immediate curation was deemed false" (375), and falseness is unacceptable once a shared, minoritarian truth has been forged. The two archival searchers experience anti-Blackness, transphobia, and class bias that renders them triply outsiders. As Mathilda begins to speak in the plural "we" regarding her experiences with Erskine-Lily, she also expands her archival interests and boldness. In considering their partnership and shared affinities, Mathilda thinks, "We had no need of substance, we'd had our fill of it" (374), pointing to the non-substantial or unsubstantiated they seek in the archive of Hermia. Once the bond is formed, they are one, and the archive of their transfixions becomes a horizon of the future rather than a tomb for the past. This is central to the praxis and non-teleology of the minor archive novel: The generic materials of the past – curated, arranged, overwritten, recalibrated, re-encoded – are deterritorialized onto a path to a different, better future. In community with the past, a particular sort of past, the future becomes habitable, imaginable. Mathilda and Erskine-Lily avoid "biographical detail" about themselves, holding to the mantra of "No talk about Life Before" (300). But the novel puts the two of them in thrall of a life not strictly before but astride their own, which ironically helps cordon off their histories before knowing each other. Life "had an unhealthy fixation with us" (375), as contemporary avatars of elegant outsiderdom, and yet they, of course, are fixated on another set of past lives. Mathilda diminishes the method, noting, "All we'd done was trace a thread of sensibility from figure to figure" (383), but this is an archival charge unavailable to those who do not share sensibilities with said figures.

Whereas Erskine-Lily and Mathilda share epistemological characteristics, their relationship is exceptional to the latter's experience at the Residency. The Residency is dominated by the figure of Garreaux and his Thought Art acolytes, a mostly theoretical endeavor that "frowned on art that sought to express *identity*" (185). In the case of Mathilda's transfixions, it is identity that becomes legible as art. Mathilda notes that her initial "fascination with Stephan Tennant . . . allowed me to embody a queer fantasy not immediately accessible" (209), and his imparted queerness is the borrowed access that leads Mathilda to the far more radical figure of Hermia. When Mathilda swaps an archived final project for her own, it of course turns out to be Hermia's, co-implicating them in a kind of archival fraud, casting doubt on the entire edifice of the place. It also renders Hermia a different sort of Transfixion, one to whom Mathilda can aspire directly as she builds up this figure through archival discovery and intervention. As the only Black woman amongst the LOTE society around Tennant, Hermia is confused for another rare figure, Josephine Baker (52), and carries herself in such a way that Mathilda remarks how "having to pass" as royalty "was so stressful" (76). Hermia is an archival figure even in life, an index for Blackness and foreign royalty, the latter a means of including her in society that was legible to the white elite. Hermia literally veils herself in many of the photos and accounts, on which Mathilda remarks, "There had, in fact, always been a little hiding wrapped up in the spectacle" (225). The meaning of the veiling changes with perceptions of Hermia's Blackness, but needless to say, Mathilda and Erskine-Lily have a different perspective from those beholding Hermia in her time. But it is finally Hermia's pursuit of beauty in and through life that is central to her transfixing, transformative power, suggesting a particular cipher for the archive into which Mathilda inserts herself. In a conversation with friend Malachi, Mathilda speculates on the ways in which Hermia persists as a figure who embodies "the fantasy regardless, in spite of, *to spite*," to "extrapolate the elegance" and "show it as a universal material," to which Malachi rejoins, "Black people consuming and creating beauty of a certain kind is still one of the most transgressive things that can happen in the West" (209). For her part, as if there were some concern, Hermia's "love of beauty" is noted to not have "diluted" her Blackness (210), and instead "Hermia's race brought an entirely different dimension to the matter of personal style" (274), a style that some viewed "as an extension of her Blackness" (275). Hermia is the minor figure of the archive, reflecting and refracting back through her minoritized counterpart in the present: the annotator, the archivist, the seeker. For Mathilda, Hermia "embodied the dreaded intersection" of "femininity, adornment and Otherness"; she was "a threat to the established framework" (276) who deployed fashion as deflection from skin color (277). She is among "exploiters of style" despite being far removed "in race, class and wealth" (270).

So besides being an index and a kind of totem for Mathilda's trying to understand her own place in the world, what does Hermia have to do with the trans minor archive novel form? As Mathilda unwinds the mystery of Hermia, she eventually brings Erskine-Lily to the grand revelation: Hermia was herself a submission of a Thought Artist, archived above the archives of the Residency, living at the behest of Garreaux's father and as a result of his fixation with her. Erskine-Lily is taken aback that Hermia's room is untouched, and not "in a library or museum ... an archive at least," to which Mathilda responds: "This is an archive, just not for the public" (342). The archive renders Hermia both permanent and secreted away, never to reach even the renown of a figure such as Tennant. Mathilda reads in a book on Black Modernisms the distinction between Stephen Tennant as "marginal" and Hermia Druitt as "marginalized," embracing "outskirt cultures" and "pursuing life's marginalia" (351). The minor subject exists, at best, in the marginalia of the majoritarian, and thus in pursuing the hidden corners of the archive carves out spaces thought to be or that intentionally are lost. Whereas the historical novel can recover and invent from the collections of various extant histories, the minor archive novel seeks out boxes of ephemera "not for the public." Hermia may, amongst the Residents and Thought Artists, be "the very first submission" to their archive, but this is only literally the case, and upon her death, that submission ceases to hold any putative weight. Instead, Hermia becomes elemental to Mathilda's ability to access identity. As a minor subject, she does so according to a variety of strategies: by identification with the past, by contrast to the phobias of those around herself, and by transgressing between the veiled and the spectacular. The minor can wield this dynamic of access in the same registers in which it wields the family, mourning, and the road – deterritorializing institutions and their domains for minor uses. In the end, the distance has collapsed completely, with Mathilda occupying Erskine-Lily's abandoned apartment and introducing herself to new Residents as Hermia. The collections are merged, and Mathilda becomes the living embodiment of this minor archive – it isn't playacting or assumption; it is absorption into an archive of minoritization, marginalization, and beauty.

What Do the Dead Collect?

Where *Confessions of the Fox* is the adventure of anti-carceral sex–gender transgression, and *LOTE* is the temporal drag of reading past marginalized identities into a present that pursues a fugitive better future, Isaac Fellman's *Dead Collections* is the eternal present of immortal – literally vampiric – eros and desire. *Fox* is an archive of abolitionisms, *LOTE* an index of race/class/gender in the brightened corners of the past, and *Dead Collections* the shadowy basement of terminal/permanent disability and the phobias that relegate subjects to them. Despite the omnipresent risks associated with his undead condition, trans masc vampire Sol is a trained and, by all accounts, careful and excellent archivist. This kind of mastery is not in development: Sol is equipped for whatever comes across his desk, comporting himself more like a morose film noir gumshoe as Elsie breezes into his life, attached to the archive of her deceased wife, a cult-famous TV writer. The archives of the Historical Society of Northern California are responsible for Sol's mortal/cisnormative life cycle, in reverse. First, they kill him: "I cursed my work, for it had been there that the accident happened. Archives are full of poisons, but I never expected to die of them" (27). The medical solution of the day is induced vampirism, and so the archive next provides a measure of shelter for Sol to live out his old/perpetual age. When he relates an archivist mentor's wisdom that "A thing is just a slow event" (8), he could be talking about himself, though it is noted that most vampires do not live long in this society, out of carelessness or suicide (if that is an appropriate term for a dead thing expiring). And so, for a vampire, "the archives were one of the safest places in the city, and I left them only in the full dark" (14), which suggests Sol desires some measure of safety under the strictures of his new existence. But of course this precaution is a reminder of a different life: "Once, I'd had other things than the archives – a home, a car, ferry trips and hikes and cups of ice cream in a hot tanned hand – but these memories had dulled next to my terror of the annihilating light" (14). The archives are refuge from annihilating terror and in opposition to creature comforts, most notably, perhaps, a home. Sol's vampirism could be read as a metaphor for archival pursuit, for disability, for the minoritized status of sex–gender dissidents, but it is best read on its own terms. Sol is trans regardless of his being a vampire, and is a skilled archivist somewhat irrespective of either of these identities.

The minor archive novel is somewhat reflexive: All minor novels are archives, no matter how speculative or premised on futurity. They index ranges of experience, identity, and history that are at once non-ephemeral and "complete" in terms of a finished work and at the same time "not public," hailing communities and affinities through methods both thematic and formal. In this case, the archive kills Sol; he is reborn as a vampire. The archive protects Sol; it reminds him of a seemingly unrecoverable past, albeit one for which he hardly mourns. The archive then presents Sol with a purpose – to unravel mysteries – and "although most mysteries begin with a dead body," the archivist reminds us "There are no dead bodies in archives," with one qualification, "except maybe for mine" (8). So Sol is a body, but "in general what you find in archives is the absence of a body, the chalk outline of a life" (8), just as in Hermia's empty room, in the evacuation of Jack's transness, Bess's brownness, Leslie Feinberg's history-less-ness. Sol sees this absence as "a terribly small hollowness within," as "It's cold in the archives, and there's nobody there. I belong in the archives. I am cold too" (8). The archive lends Sol, at least for a time, a sense of belonging.

Elsie is a different sort of archive, bringing to Sol a collection from a piece of her past and a longing for Sol that links him back to corporeality and life through sex and desire. But Elsie also brings community and care, an object for Sol's history and skill and a subject for her own love and burgeoning sense of sex–gender dissonance. As the two of them experiment with their fleshly desires, Elsie demands Sol drink her blood, resulting in both orgasms and " the kick of shame – good shame, the shame of getting what you need" (66). This exsanguination is a deep, bodily connection, heating Sol up as if he were alive. When he suggests that "archives run on longing" (61), his own existence as an archive of death and coldness seems to bar him from certain bodily expressions of longing. But upon meeting Elsie and being confronted with the archive's mysterious, super/natural ooze, Sol lives out the result of an archive of longing being filled with collections of communitarian relation: "You make less to archive once you get what you want" (61). Elsie catalogs what Sol has gotten that he wants, noting "you've done so many things with your life," among them, mastering classical "piano, the archives, transitioning. You've done things that most people wouldn't even think could be jobs or – ways of living. Or possible" (121). Sol is the dead person whose skin can get hot, the archivist who can cure Eidolism (the diagnosis of the ooze), the trans masc vampire who can maneuver between all three and win the heretofore unimaginable object of his desire. The link to the past, though, is the haunting of having been alive at all.

Sol reflects "on the things my hands remembered," and states from a position of some authority, "My body is an archive" (127). In ruminating on this "not new" idea, Sol justifies the central thematic link of the novel: "People who aren't archivists miss the ways that archives are quite specifically vampiric," the metaphor continuing that Sol is "essentially . . . a dead body on life support" and "archives are the same – dead information provided with artificial blood" (127). This is perhaps the ultimate minor archive effect; information and material deemed unworthy of compilation, catalog, and preservation become an embodied archive – generational and transhistorical, but also fungible and subject to qualification as situations demand or solicit. Where the historical novel is concerned with accounting for the past, the minor archive novel regards the past being accountable to the present. Its archival principles are centered on memory – even when that memory is invented, it is experienced. Sol is "still half thinking about myself as an archive" (131) as he considers Elsie's blood being incorporated into that archive. So Sol transitions, which is not to say progresses/develops/grows, from a professional-identitarian sense of himself as archivist to a relational-embodied sense of objecthood. He comes "to see myself as an archival item more than an archivist: weak, crumbling, and in need of a very specific environment to survive" (158). But Elsie de-objectifies him. Just as Bess brings Jack into history, and Voth orients that history in a way that is legible to trans abolitionist presents/futures, Elsie reorients Sol as archive rather than archival object.

The antagonists of *Dead Collections* are strikingly similar to those of the other archive novels in this Element: corporate (in the form of phobic coworkers and the medical industrial complex that has rendered Sol walking dead), natural (the sun), and supernatural (the alchemical magic of the substance in *Fox* or the Transfixion rituals of *LOTE* become the oozing archives here). The "sap" (26) is the antithesis of good archival practice, though Sol notes that "tears are liquids too," and their presence is proof that "you can't keep everything out of the archives" (27). Nonetheless, "archives are all crunch" (59), by their very nature comprised of decay and degradation: "Archives really are trash" (59).

Institutionalization – and The Novel can institutionalize as well – renders this trash, if not always treasure, at least worthy of a catalog number and a relatively permanent place. But this trash results in a measure of "glee ... to find out about all these old traumas and dramas" (59). It is "one of the pleasures of being a night archivist" to "get to read the things in a way that people in the archives during the day never do" (58). To slightly reframe this sentiment: The minor archive is the opportunity to read history in a way that the phobic public institutions do not care to, and could not decode even if they did. When Sol finally solves the Eidolism, it is the simplest archival solution: Process the oozing collection(s). Sol notes that most of the archives he's "known have been mostly backlog" (155). All the more so for the minoritized, where the trash may not even make it to the status of backlog, until there is an archivist who cares to open a collection. In this instance, it requires a vampire who discovers their own archival nature to clear the backlog. Sol lays out the terms of the problem to which he will devote his professional life: "How little people know about vampires, how little they know about archives, and how little they know about the undiscovered country from whose bourn no traveler returns" (156). Sol seems to take on the role of guide, but the fulfillment he derives is from the release of these backlogs, the dramas and traumas, the surfacing of the buried – a perpetual practice that will perhaps reveal territories from which travelers return via what they leave behind. This makes Sol "an exorcist," though "it feels like I'm still an archivist" (178). But he is also perfectly suited for this work, requiring limited sustenance and money only for "gas and a few clothes" (178). This is one of the few instances, at the very end of the novel, in which Sol makes reference to his sex–gender identity as part of his being suited for this archive/archivist work: "I'm a trans man," he quips. "I only shop at Uniqlo anyway, where the sleeves don't go down to my fingertips" (178). He is embodied archival desire, requiring essentially nothing other than the material itself, the clearing of backlog and the exercising of his own archival longing.

The Trans Minor Archive Novel

Arondekar seeks after readings that productively juxtapose "the archive's fiction effects (the archive as a system of representation) alongside its truth effects (the archive as material with 'real' consequences) – not as incommensurate, but as agonistically coconstitutive of each other" (4). I, conversely, attempt to register fiction's "archive effects," the ways in which it uses and constitutes an archive of narrative content and form. These are affective effects, hailing communities through experiential knowledge and muddling majoritarian accounting and cataloging through disidentification. In this way, I wonder with Joynt and Schilt, "How can emotional responses – responses that are often excluded from many academic modes of information dissemination – be harnessed to produce new lines of inquiry?" (636). One way might be through Edwards's concept of counter-archival reading, a trans minor hermeneutics that could deploy generic convention, for instance, in service of revealing its normativizing limitations and anti-normative potentials. Edwards writes, "A self-reflective counterarchival reading stays alert to the desires, demands, and dangers of recuperative projects, asking, for example: Might current trans* archival consolidation erase the ways in which (il)legibility operated, often violently, on the bodies called to bear that (il)legibility in archival classification?" (653). One way to resist this erasure, or at least to offer means of decoding how phobic public institutions enact it, is through the minor archive novel's inventions and innovations. When Edwards goes on to ask of the archive, "What kinds of 'trans*' are we seeking? And why?" (654), the minor archive novel can show rather than tell, offering ways of being and ways of archiving alike. Late in *Fox*, Voth notes that "History does not progress, but rather piles and strews" whereas the archive constitutes "An impossible, ghostly archaeology – unexcavatable and haunting" (310n). Where the historical novel excavates, tracking histories ("faithful" or speculative, "authentic" or fabulated), the trans minor archive novel inhabits the archaeology, revealing the minoritized subject as renovating their own minoritarian habitus from the piles and strews.

6 TransGeneric

Transgeneric

The preceding sections, in their relative discreteness, may give an incomplete sense of the TransGeneric. In this brief conclusion, I want to emphasize slippages, mutability, the dare-I-say utopian potentiality of trans minor genre play in fiction. Deleuze and Guattari (*Kafka: Toward a Minor Literature*) noted of the minor, "From one genre of text to another, there are interactions, reinvestments, exchanges, and so on" (39), and indeed, I have selected four genre sites that offer each of these. In his analysis of form in Feinberg's *Stone Butch Blues*, Jay Prosser suggested that Feinberg's novel "produces an alternative generic form – a trans-genre: a text as between genres as its subject is between genders" (178). In retrospect, I find this parallelism a bit too cute; measuring the degree to which Jess is "between genders" is not a particularly productive exercise. But what Prosser may be driving at with his "trans-genre" is what Feinberg hirself noted regarding the facticity/realness of hir minoritarian fiction. Writing about another autobiographically inflected work of minor fiction, Qiu Miaojin's *Last Words from Montmartre*, Larissa Heinrich ("Begin Anywhere") notes that the work deploys "transgender aspects of the narrator's identity to reinforce, to mirror, to model, and to construct what is also a transgenre literary *form*" (162). Similar to Prosser's analysis, Heinrich's assessment centers on transgender subjectivity challenging formal generic boundaries. Finally, Salah ("Transgender and Transgenre Writing") notes that "'Trans genre,' which is both a pun and a neologism, associates cross-genre writing with writing that interferes with or intervenes in the classification of gender" (182). For my part, *TransGenre* attempts to turn this formulation inside out: using genre reading practices to both expose cisheteronormative underpinnings of forms of fiction as well as strange and minor trans uses thereof. As I consider some of the slippages between genres, performing a more literally transgeneric set of readings, I want to bear in mind two questions posed by the theorists in this Element. First, Beebee's query of what we are reading when we read generic instability. If each of the preceding sections deterritorializes and reappropriates elements of its constitutive genre, then we are indeed reading for generic instability. Second, Salah's consideration of what "remains a contested question: How does writing in between or across genres of humanity actualize our collective being?" (191). Thinking of literary genre and form as reflecting or refracting genres of humanity takes us back closer to Stone's formulation of trans as a set of embodied texts, ripe for productive disruption.

We began this inquiry with *Nevada* as exemplar of the difficulties of a minor road novel, not least that deeming it such threatens to overwrite the first half of the novel! In that first half, Maria's domesticity is furtive and doomed from the onset; the novel opens with an abortive attempt at a faked orgasm, the telos of Maria's dissociation during sex with a partner who exists in Maria's life primarily as a counter to all of her pretense and (often self-protective) self-delusion. But the road novel half also ends with sexual uncertainty, James wondering if there's room in the car to receive oral sex from his partner, Nicole, who has picked him up from the end of the Reno adventure with Maria. These parallel scenes of sexual frustration bookend a novel premised on Maria's cyclical journey away from Steph and the New York life she's cultivated, and toward James and the impossible utopia of his tutelage into trans womanhood. The moment when Maria's quest for irresponsibility runs aground of the imaginary of community and a kind of elder/educator relationship – that is to say, chosen family – the road novel falls apart.

It is hardly coincidental that the mourning novels of this Element share territory with the chosen family novels and vice versa. But the disjunction of their Venn diagrams is at least as significant as their overlap. In *The Thirty Names of Night*, Nadir's search for Laila's (and, by extension, Nadir's mother's) bird is driven by loss, as is Jules's road trip with B's ashes in *And Then the Gray Heaven*, as is the curation of the *Little Blue Encyclopedia (for Vivian)*. The mourning novels each challenge grievability and majoritarian concepts of memorialization and persistence of community and, yes, chosen family. But whereas the chosen family novels are often suffused with loss and reasons to mourn as well – Mei has lost most of her biofamily in *Small Beauty*, the *Fierce Femmes* have lost the First Femme, among others, Wendy and the other femmes lose Sophie in *Little Fish*, Reese loses Amy, then her baby in *Detransition, Baby* – they center on the choice element of chosen family. No one chooses to lose a part of their community or family in these novels; minoritarian agency is enacted in how community and family are maintained, reformulated, or abandoned. Nevertheless, the idea of mourning as more anticipatable or even foreordained for minoritized subject positions (in these novels, those include migrant, disabled, racialized, and classed, in addition to sex–gender) is consistently played against reflections on relationality: one-to-one, often homosocial or romantic relationships, small units melding mutual aid and familial care, and broader communitarian reflections on transness, queerness, and other concurrently embodied marginalized identities.

In a very real, formal sense, though, each of these preceding genres is imbricated with the minor archive. Beans Velocci ("Denaturing Cisness") argues for deploying "trans history as a method" for which "What is required next is another fundamental model of trans history, one that focuses on the systemic absurdity of static and binary gender and sex classification" (112). This focus and methodology include "an alternative logic of how sex and gender function, which complements but also exceeds trans history as an archive of particular, recognizable objects" (112). Even at their most fantastic, novels are made up of the particular and recognizable, and we could argue that trans minor novels are marked in their particularity and how they signal community. But Velocci is focused on actual archival research wherein "Trans people become visible in archives because of behaviors that are supposed to be exceptional, and everyone else is presumed to be cis" (116). If the trans minor archive novel is an answer to the (cis) majoritarian historical novel, then part of the answer is its construction of its own archival practices, materials, and conclusions. Minor literature archives and indexes narratives, and trans minor literature often reveals the behaviors of cis subjects as exceptional and absurd. But for this Element, we can consider what kinds of archives are implicated in the trans minor road, mourning, and chosen family novel genres.

The generic conventions of the road are on one, rather superficial axis indexed according to where the traveler is along their path. There is perhaps a prehistory, an initial shoving off, and then the time "on the road." For *Nevada*, the prehistory is half the novel, and the other half is a single stop along the way. Furthermore, through the brief glimpses of Maria's history that we are given, the narrative suggests she is in fact at the end of one track of her development (she is an expert in her own mind at being trans) and not about to come to any grand, or at least lasting, revelations about the others that preoccupy her (relationships, career, her writing). The road itself becomes mirage, as there is nowhere to run to, really. Perhaps in this way Binnie meets Kerouac, but Maria's archive of experiences and sensibilities regarding her trans womanhood speak to communities who share those experiences (privileged though some elements of them may be) in a way that Dean and Sal's are a more diffuse, "generational" code. They record a moment, where Maria records a perspective.

Not dissimilarly, the archive of trans minor mourning is one of preservation and finding value in the mourning and its persistence, rather than as a means to the end of "being over it." Mourning is omnipresent in these novels, creating a three-dimensional archive of memory, embodied affects/effects, and narrative. Minor mourning founds, deepens, and rips through community formation according to how the archive is encountered, and the artifacts of majoritarian conceptions of mourning (anger, acceptance, forgiveness) are absented, attenuated, or scrambled. This makes for a messy archive – lots of backlog – which is perhaps why each of the novels featured in this section include a project of some variety to bring order (which of course the novel itself does, as well).

Biofamilies are histories of genealogy and structured kinship and responsibility. Shared lineage and codependence, distance or closeness measured against expectation of culturally defined roles all lead to expectations of the field of possibility for narrative specifically centered on family. In certain ways, then, minor chosen family novels could be an archive of distinction, recording all the ways in which having the agency to choose one's kin, and to alter or revoke the terms of that kinship, are distinct from or similar to biofamily. But each of these family novels is a particular kind of archive, reading trans subjectivity and experience against a backdrop of different sorts of family relationships, often (indirectly) problematizing the simple arc of a before-during-after of transition. *Small Beauty* is perhaps the most direct in this regard, deterritorializing memories of biofamily onto loneliness and trans becoming. Its archive is of moments of joy and trauma, some violent, some quotidian. *Little Fish* is also somewhat an archive of retrospect, reconstructing experiences with the absent family member, but also the sense of moments in the present piling and strewing, with chosen familial relationships (and at this point, Wendy has chosen to have biological father Ben in her life, as his daughter) as the index of trans womanhood. By the end of the novel, we may understand Wendy's frame of reference and her attempts to cope with the brutal everyday, but we hardly have anything like a history. *Fierce Femmes* is most linear in this regard, as we track the narrator from pre-transition in her biofamily home through to having left behind both that family and the ones she has chosen. But this multimedia novel is itself an archive of poems, letters, and supernatural anecdotes cut into the main narrative. Thom's narrator chooses to include a careful accounting of relationships with each member of her past and present families, and her characterization is predominately through how they interact with her. The novel is thus as archive of sensations are reactions, reflections on trans becoming and self-determination. Finally, *Detransition, Baby* is the trans minor archive of "formative" family decisions, always justifying with whom to surround oneself and what comprises minoritarian community. Reese, Amy, and Ames theorize de/transition and being trans versus doing trans as an archive of their histories with one another. In signature style (similar to her earlier *Infect Your Friends and Loved Ones*), Peters jumps back and forward in time, destabilizing cause-and-effect presumptions regarding de/transition and the notion of "family planning." Peters has arranged the archive of narrative events in a manner that does not use chronology as its organizing principle.

Finally, reading the works I have included in the archive novel section itself through their other genre resources reveals further flexibility in minor deterritorialization. *Confessions of the Fox* performs an interesting trick with both mourning and chosen family: The frame narrator at once mourns the loss of a foundational romantic relationship and at the same time finds chosen family in the archive itself. The novel deterritorializes history onto the fungible territory of collective memory and reclaimed pasts. *LOTE* performs a similar operation, but in a much more recent history, such that its archival searchers can find family in each other as well as their connection to a lived history. When Mathilda become Hermia, she converts mourning into embodiment, a transmogrification unapparent to those who did not know her before, and the novel undercuts the "before" with each next revelation of Hermia's life and work. And *Dead Collections* adds in a literal romance of the archive, the detritus of the past animated and enlivened through restiveness and a desire to be cataloged. Sol and his paramour renarrativize their histories as a shared becoming, a deterritorialization of death as beginning rather than end. The courtship novel baked into the narrative is perhaps the least remarkable aspect of the work in its trajectory, save for the ways in which it appears to literally revive the dead.

Transgeneric reading practices seek out the raw materials of genre and remap their territories for minor uses, ways of narrativizing experience through dreams of the major language. But these dreams are not aspirational or assimilative; rather they are demands for community and space for communities both broader and narrower. To understand transness as a set of embodied texts is a minoritarian understanding, an archive that is not for the public, or at least not every public. Rather than reflecting on how real life defies genre, we might think of genre defying real life, and minor literature as a way to wield its uncanny correspondences and potentials for radical deterritorialization. Trans minor literature can at once demand its own functions and promiscuously operate the forms of the major, undercutting fixed and linearly developing sense of sex–gender, identity formation, and embodiment. These destabilizations are the grounds for the revolutionary potentiality of the minor: to question the dictates and facticity of the comfortable, phobic majoritarian through its great (and established) forms.

Works Cited

Arondekar, Anjali (2009) *For the Record: On Sexuality and the Colonial Archive in India*. Durham, NC: Duke University Press.

Awkward-Rich, Cameron (2022) *The Terrible We: Thinking with Trans Maladjustment*. Durham, NC: Duke University Press.

Bawrashi, Anis, and Reiff, Mary Jo (2010) *Genre: An Introduction to History, Theory, Research, and Pedagogy*. Anderson, SC: Parlor Press.

Beebee, Thomas (1994) *The Ideology of Genre: A Comparative Study of Generic Instability*. State College: Pennsylvania State University Press.

Binnie, Imogen (2013) *Nevada*. Brooklyn, NY: Topside Press.

Butler, Judith (1988) Performative Acts and Gender Constitution: An Essay in Phenomenology and Feminist Theory. *Theatre Journal*, 40(4), 519–531. www.jstor.org/stable/3207893?origin=JSTOR-pdf.

Butler, Judith (2004) *Precarious Life: The Powers of Mourning and Violence*. New York: Verso.

Califia, Patrick (1997) *Sex Changes: The Politics of Transgenderism*. Hoboken, NJ: Cleis.

Candelario, Ginetta E. B. (2022) Editor's Introduction. *Meridians: Feminism, Race, Transnationalism*, 21(2), 299–301.

Culler, Jonathan (2009). Lyric, History, and Genre. *New Literary History*, 40(4), 879–899. www.jstor.org/stable/40666452.

Deleuze, Gilles, and Félix Guattari ([1975] 1986) *Kafka: Toward a Minor Literature*, translated by Dana Polan. Minneapolis: University of Minnesota Press.

Derrida, Jacques (1980) The Law of Genre. *Glyph* 7, 202–232.

Derrida, Jacques (1995) *Archive Fever: A Freudian Impression*. Chicago, IL: University of Chicago Press.

Devitt, Amy (1993) Generalizing about Genre: New Conceptions of an Old Concept. *Composition and Communication* 44(4), 573–586. https://doi.org/10.2307/358391.

Digital Transgender Archive (2020) About. www.digitaltransgenderarchive.net/about/overview.

Dimock, Wai Chee (2006) Genre as World System: Epic and Novel on Four Continents. *Narrative* 14(1), 85–101.

Edwards, Rebekah (2015) "This Is Not a Girl": A Trans* Archival Reading. *Transgender Studies Quarterly* 2(4), 650–665.

Emerson, Caryl, and Morson, Gary Saul (1990) *Mikhail Bakhtin: Creation of a Prosaics*. Palo Alto, CA: Stanford University Press.

Feinberg, Leslie (1993) *Stone Butch Blues*. New York: Alyson Books.

Feinberg, Leslie (1996) *Transgender Warriors*. New York: Beacon.

Felker-Martin, Gretchen (2022) *Manhunt*. New York: Tor Nightfire.

Fellman, Isaac (2022) *Dead Collections*. New York: Penguin.

Fleischmann, T. (2019) *Time Is the Thing a Body Moves Through*. Minneapolis, MN: Coffee House Press.

Frye, Northrop (1971) *Anatomy of Criticism: Four Essays*. Princeton, NJ: Princeton University Press.

Giles, Harry Josephine (2020) F-Words: The Many Languages of Transfeminism. *Engender*. September 28. www.engender.org.uk/news/blog/f-words-the-many-languages-of-transfeminism.

Gill-Peterson, Jules (2024) *A Short History of Trans Misogyny*. New York: Verso.

Hammes, Aaron (2024) Minor Literature as Trans Literature. In Douglas A. Vakoch and Sabine Sharp (eds.) *The Routledge Handbook of Transgender Literature*. New York: Routledge, 448–458.

Hartman, Sadiya (2008) Venus in Two Acts. *Small Axe*, 12(2), 1–14.

Heartscape, Porpentine Charity (2023) *Serious Weakness*. Self-published.

Heinrich, Larissa (2012) Begin Anywhere: Transgender and Transgenre Desire in Qiu Miaojin's *Last Words from Montmartre*. In Chiang, H. (ed.) *Transgender China*. New York: Palgrave Macmillan, 161–181.

Heyam, Kit (2022) *Before We Were Trans*. London: Seal Press.

Israeli-Nevo, Atalia (2017) Taking (My) Time: Temporality in Transition, Queer Delays and Being (in the) Present. *Somatechnics*, 7(1), 34–49.

Jacques, Juliet (2019) Variations: Transgender Memoir, Theory and Fiction. University of Sussex thesis. https://sussex.figshare.com/articles/thesis/Variations_transgender_memoir_theory_and_fiction/23470952/1/files/41179544.pdf.

Jameson, Fredric (1975) Magical Narratives: Romance as Genre. *New Literary History*, 7(1), 135–163.

Jarboe, Julian K (2020) *Everyone on the Moon Is Essential Personnel*. Amherst, MA: Lethe.

Joukhadar, Zeyn (2021) *The Thirty Names of Night*. New York: Washington Square.

Joynt, Chase, and Schilt, Kristen (2015) Anxiety at the Archive. *Transgender Studies Quarterly*, 2(4), 635–644.

Katz, R. E. (2021) *And Then the Gray Heaven*. Ann Arbor, MI: Dzanc Books.

Kerouac, Jack (1999) *On the Road*. New York: Penguin Classics.

Kübler-Ross, Elisabeth (2014) *On Death and Dying: What the Dying Have to Teach Doctors, Nurses, Clergy and Their Own Families*. New York: Scribner.

Lake, Joss (2021) *Future Feeling*. New York: Soft Skull.

Lavery, Grace (2023) *Pleasure and Efficacy: Of Pen Names, Cover Versions, and Other Trans Techniques*. Princeton, NJ: Princeton University Press.

Lawlor, Andrea (2019) *Paul Takes the Form of a Mortal Girl*. New York: Vintage.

Lukács, Georg (1983) *The Historical Novel*. Lincoln: University of Nebraska Press.

Malatino, Hil (2022) *Side Affects: On Being Trans and Feeling Bad*. Minneapolis: University of Minnesota Press.

Mccaslin, Charlotte (2023) Ofrenda. *Ofrenda*, Roselit Bone, Get Loud Recordings.

McDonnell, M. Z. (2019) *Poet, Prophet, Fox: The Tale of Sinnach the Seer*. Nyack, NY: Moose Maple Press.

Milks, Megan (2021) *Margaret and the Mystery of the Missing Body*. New York: Amethyst Editions.

Miller, Carolyn R. (1984) Genre as Social Action. *Quarterly Journal of Speech* 70, 151–167.

Muñoz, José Esteban (1999) *Disidentifications: Queers of Color and the Performance of Politics*. Minneapolis: University of Minnesota Press.

Peters, Torrey (2021) *Detransition, Baby*. New York: One World.

Plante, Hazel Jane (2019) *Little Blue Encyclopedia (for Vivian)*. Montreal, QC: Metonymy.

Plante, Hazel Jane (2023) *Any Other City*. Vancouver, BC: Arsenal Pulp.

Plett, Casey (2018) *Little Fish*. Vancouver, BC: Arsenal Pulp.

Proseer, Jay (1998) *Second Skins*. New York: Columbia University Press.

Raha, Nat (2017) Transfeminine Brokenness, Radical Transfeminism. *South Atlantic Quarterly*, 116 (3), 632–646.

Rawson, K. J. (2014) Archive. *Transgender Studies Quarterly*, 1(1–2), 24–26.

Roberts, Ronald Suresh (2002) Keeping the Self: The Novelist as (Self-)Archivist. In Hamilton, C., Harris, V., Taylor, J., Pickover, M., Reid, G., and Saleh, R. (eds.) *Refiguring the Archive*. New York: Springer, 301–322.

Rosenberg, Jordy (2019) *Confessions of the Fox*. New York: One World.

Salah, Trish (2021) Transgender and Transgenre Writing. In Miller, J. (ed.) *The Cambridge Companion to Twenty-First Century American Fiction*. Cambridge: Cambridge University Press, 174–195.

Stone, Sandy (2006) The Empire Strikes Back. In Stryker, S. and Whittle, S. (eds.) *The Transgender Studies Reader*. New York: Routledge, 221–235.

Stryker, Susan (2006) My Words to Victor Frankenstein above the Village of Chamounix: Performing Transgender Rage. In Stryker, S. and Whittle, S. (eds.) *The Transgender Studies Reader*. New York: Routledge, 244–256.

Stryker, Susan (2008) *Transgender History.* New York: Seal Press.

Thom, Kai Cheng (2016) *Fierce Femmes and Notorious Liars.* Montreal, QC: Metonymy Press.

Thompson, Hunter S. (1998) *Fear and Loathing in Las Vegas: A Savage Journey to the Heart of the American Dream.* New York: Vintage.

Thornton, Jeanne (2021) *Summer Fun.* New York: Soho Press.

Van Zyl, Susan (2002) Psychoanalysis and the Archive: Derrida's *Archive Fever.* In Hamilton, C., Harris, V., Taylor, J., Pickover, M., Reid, G., and Saleh, R. (eds.) *Refiguring the Archive.* New York: Springer, 39–60.

Velocci, Beans (2024) Denaturing Cisness, or, Toward Trans History as Method. In Heaney, E. (ed.) *Feminism against Cisness.* Durham, NC: Duke University Press, 108–133.

Von Reinhold, Shola (2020) *LOTE.* London: Jacaranda.

Von Reinhold, Shola (2021) Interview. *Lucy Writers.* https://lucywritersplat form.com/2021/06/01/interview-with-shola-von-reinhold-it-felt-like-her mia-fabulated-herself-out-of-the-archive.

Whitehead, Joshua (2018) *Jonny Appleseed.* Vancouver, BC: Arsenal Pulp.

wilson-yang, jia qing (2016) *Small Beauty.* Montreal, QC: Metonymy Press.

Cambridge Elements ≡

Feminism and Contemporary Critical Theory

Jennifer Cooke
Loughborough University

Jennifer Cooke is Reader in Contemporary Literature and Theory at Loughborough University. She's author of *Contemporary Feminist Life-Writing: The New Audacity* (2020) and editor of *The New Feminist Literary Studies* (2020), *Scenes of Intimacy: Reading, Writing and Theorizing Contemporary Literature* (2013), and a special issue of *Textual Practice* on challenging intimacies and psychoanalysis (September 2013). Her first monograph is *Legacies of Plague in Literature, Theory and Film* (2009). Her research interests lie in theories of intimacy, the affective turn and theories of the emotions, queer and feminist theories, and contemporary literature. She chaired the Gendered Lives Research Group from 2015 to 2020.

Amber Jamilla Musser
CUNY Graduate Center

Amber Jamilla Musser is Professor of English at the CUNY Graduate Center. She is the author of *Sensational Flesh: Race, Power, and Masochism* (2014), *Sensual Excess: Queer Femininity and Brown Jouissance* (2018), and co-editor with Kadji Amin and Roy Peréz of a special issue of *ASAP Journal* on Queer Form (May 2017). She has also published extensively, including essays in *Feminist Theory, differences, Social Text, GLQ, and Women and Performance* on the intersections of critical race theory, sexuality studies, queer of color critique, black feminisms, and aesthetics.

Juno Jill Richards
Yale University

Juno Jill Richards is Associate Professor in English and affiliated faculty in Women, Gender, & Sexuality Studies at Yale University. They are the author of *The Fury Archives: Female Citizenship, Human Rights, and the International Avant-Gardes* (2020) and a co-author of *The Ferrante Letters: An Experiment in Collective Criticism* (2020). Their research focuses on queer/trans archives, social reproduction, critical legal theory, queer feminist science studies, disability justice, and 20th/21st century literature.

About the Series

Elements in Feminism and Contemporary Critical Theory provides a forum for interdisciplinary feminist scholarship that speaks directly to the contemporary moment. Grounded in queer, trans, antiracist, and intersectional feminist traditions, the series expands familiar paradigms of academic writing, locating new methods and modes to account for transformational feminist politics today.

Cambridge Elements ☰

Feminism and Contemporary Critical Theory

Elements in the Series

A full series listing is available at: www.cambridge.org/EFCT

Printed in the United States
by Baker & Taylor Publisher Services